The Grail Path

Achieving Mystical Transformation
for the Creative and Emotional Person

Mischa V Alyea

Aashni
Spiritual Living

Aashni Spiritual Living

1530 NE 51st Street

Kansas City, MO 64118

Website: www.AashniSpiritualLiving.com

E-mail: info@AashniSpiritualLiving.com

Printed and bound in the United States

ISBN-13: 978-0692558836
ISBN-10: 0692558837

THIS BOOK IS **NOT** FOR EVERYONE

The practices and processes that I will describe are meant for creative and emotional persons. The old science defined these people as being right-brained. The newest scientific data has defined these people as having brains that run on the Imagination Circuit. Basically, these people naturally operate from the heart and intuition. They store information and understanding in, and through, their emotional circuitry. They are natural givers, they can feel the emotions of others, and they can naturally intuit creative solutions.

TABLE OF CONTENTS

Mythological symbols
come from the psyche
and speak to the psyche;
they do not spring from
or refer to historical events.
They are not to be read
as newspaper reports
of things that,
once upon a time,
actually happened."

Joseph Campbell,
"The Interpretation of
Symbolic Forms,"
The Mythic Dimension,
p. 198

INTRODUCTION

I believe that I am the only person who is jealous of the Biblical character Job. Job suffered the complete breakdown of his inner world only once. To date, I have experienced this phenomenon on three different occasions. In every case, the person who initiated me, which involved opening my base chakra and allowing the Divine Power of Kundalini to rise within my spiritual system, was well meaning. They truly believed that what they were doing would benefit my spiritual development. The result, however, was that my inner world was shattered. Every spiritual attainment that I had worked months and years to achieve was ripped from my soul. The complete psychological devastation brought about an all-embracing despair that took much effort on my part to keep from committing suicide. The diagram below is a rendition of a drawing from my meditation journal. It depicts the shattering effects when the Divine Power of Kundalini is allowed to rise within a spiritual system that has already begun The Grail Path.

This is why I wrote this book. No one should have to experience physical agony or gamble the possibility of irreversible psychological harm to achieve inner transformation. The process of spiritual transformation should be a natural process of growth and increasing wellbeing. Catastrophic psychological events are completely unnecessary when there is a full understanding of the **Two** Divine Energies and how they operate. You'll see what I mean by this shortly.

During the years of researching, in hundreds of books, I've learned that my physical and psychological setbacks were minor compared to what others have suffered. While I still suffer from a few relatively minor physical ailments, I have been fortunate to regain my mental faculties. I have heard stories of people who went to an energy healer for a simple energy balancing and were reverted all the way back to infanthood. They could not remember how to walk, talk, or even control their bowels. They were literally born again and had to rebuild their lives from a blank slate. Some never recovered memories prior to initiation. Others, like the famous philosopher Friedrich Nietzsche, never recovered from the psychological incapacitation. Nietzsche spent the last 10 years of his life in a semi-vegetative state after declaring that God was dead. I have also witnessed people who have become clinically insane all because the wrong energy was transmitted into their spiritual system.

The problems that take place when the spiritual system is overloaded with Kundalini include constant, medically unexplainable pain, hypersensitivity to sounds and emotional environments, mental fog and confusion, and a hopelessness that is so deep that thoughts of suicide have to be continually battled. When the shattering power of the Divine Power of Kundalini reaches an undifferentiated mind, confusion reigns. Clarity of the mind is replaced with indecision, doubt, and lack of self-confidence.

The first time I was initiated was the most severe. I actually woke up the next day with an amnesia that lasted for about two weeks. I felt completely dead inside. The bubbling vibrancy of life was replaced with an itching and agony that baffled the medical community. All memories stored in the emotional circuits of my spiritual system were burned off by the inferno created by the uprising of Kundalini. I did not know who I was or who the other people in the house were. I knew the names of my husband and children. Other than that they were just random strangers to me. My home felt like a place out of my distant past that no longer had any meaning to my current situation.

I could not, and still do not, remember any of the events that occurred during the evening of my first initiation. I have been told that I was given a spiritual name, but I don't remember that either. I am aware that a spiritual name is used to remind you of the supposedly wonderful initiation experience, but considering the horrific aftermath of my initiation, I do not ever want to know that spiritual name. For me, *Life* is spiritual. *Everything* embodies and expresses the divine. Jesus never changed his name. The attainment of The Christ was tacked on to Jesus' birth name like Ph.D. and M.D. are today. The same was true for Mary the Virgin, who became Mary the Mother. The Apostle John and Mary the Magdalene are more examples of those who received special attainment but did not change their birth name.

In this book I will describe how myth uses physical events as metaphor to explain spiritual experiences. The horror of a Kundalini overload has been fully detailed in the myths and parables of the ancients. We find the progression of devastation in the Biblical book of Exodus. The ten plagues of Moses represent the events that happen during a Kundalini overload experience. At first, the river of sustaining water turns red. Then the fish that swam in the water, die. Frogs escape the poisoned water and flood the surrounding land. Next, is a continual buzzing in the ears of imaginary gnats and flies. Larger beasts die. Then comes the plague of physical boils on both people and animals. Grace is hardened into hail that destroys instead of nourishes. It brings the locusts that kill the crops of life sustaining grain. The sky goes black for three days. The final plague is the death of the divine child or first-born son.

We see a similar progression of the devastation of a Kundalini upsurge in the Stations of the Cross. When the Divine Power of Kundalini is ignited in a creative or emotional personality, Life becomes a Way of Sorrows. It begins with the whipping. The pain then burdens us as if we are dragging a heavy object along the way. There are a few bright points when others help us for small periods of time through the stumbles and falls. When the aura is stripped of its light, the agony of the hands and feet begins. As the crucifixion continues, we struggle for each breath. We cry out to God asking, "Why have you forsaken me?" Then we die. Resurrection cannot happen without Grace. If the Kundalini continues to be ignited, then the abject despair can lead to insanity or suicide. The average crucifixion lasted days. This scenario of torment can last an entire life. It can kill the soul of a person who is by nature creative or emotional.

The myths of the ancient Greeks are filled with the tales of rape. I have to say, from personal experience, that the explosive uprising of the Kundalini through the base chakra in a virginal spiritual system does feel like rape and includes all the feelings of violation and humiliation that rape brings to the table. The white robed aura is stripped off as the Kundalini explodes through the base chakra, and an agony that is reminiscent of a horse whipping then flows up the spine that turns into a blackout of the spirit. The strength of the Kundalini determines how much emotional memory is wiped. A small and weak uprising will create a minor fog, while a large and strong uprising has the capacity to completely wipe the mind of all memory.

The ancients feared eclipses because they represented the blocking of the natural flow of spiritual energies. For those who are sensitive to the divine energies this blockage can be physically felt. The Super Blood Moon of September 27, 2015 was quite distressing for me. The eclipse caused a very strong Kundalini surge in my spiritual system. I was able to ride out the event because I knew it would be short lived. The moment I felt the upwelling, I performed spiritual practices to counteract this surge so that it would not cause damage to my inner being.

Not everyone is negatively affected by the initiation of the Divine Power of Kundalini. I have seen those whose lives changed for the better after initiation, even to the point where their face glowed so bright that you could be blinded by their enlightened presence. ***So, the rise of Kundalini is not a bad thing for everyone.*** If this is so, then why did I, and many others, suffer in such debilitating ways?

4

The Divine Power of Kundalini

can both kill and it can heal.

The same is true of the Divine Power of Grace.

The big question is: Under what circumstances do different divine powers kill? Under what circumstances do divine powers heal? The ancients believed that the differences were designated by the sexes. In ancient times, women were banned from participating in esoteric cults that venerated and raised the Kundalini within the spiritual system. The Mithraic mysteries are a prime example. Today, the Freemasons also refuse to admit women, for good reason. Genesis 3:15 states that the snake, a common symbol for the Power of Kundalini, will cause fear in women.

Today, we know that just because you are a woman does not necessarily mean that you are a creative and emotional personality. There are many highly intellectual women in the world. So, I dug into the psychological differences and found this very simple answer:

The spiritual needs of the individual

are determined by the way the brain operates.

Modern science and new technologies can look deeper into the body's structure to determine the differences between people. The old science used the analogy of right-brained and left-brained to designate the differences between intellectual and creative-emotional people. Today, with the advent of brain scanning technology, science has revealed that the brain does not light up on just one side or the other. It works in networks or circuits. There are three distinct circuits in the brain.

They are:

- **The Executive Attention Network**, which governs focus and linear thinking.

- **The Imagination Network**, which governs creativity, empathy (emotions), and running mental simulations.

- **The Internal Salience Network**, which governs inner awareness and outer movements.

Your mind really does run in circles. By running day after day on the same path, it creates a deeply grooved track that takes spiritual work and conscious effort to escape. It is unknown if we are born with a preference to one of these circuits or if our life experiences engrain this preference. I think it is a combination of both.

In order for a creative-emotional person to benefit from spiritual practice, they need to strengthen the Executive Attention Network. By redirecting the feelings away from dramatic re-runs and endless possibilities, the creative-emotional person can get off the emotional roller coaster. Stress reduction and calmness are the natural result of choosing a spiritual path that strengthens the weaker circuit of the brain.

If you are a creative or emotional person or are a psychological counselor or a trained spiritual advisor that guides creative or emotional people then this book is for you. It will explain:

- Why the ego-killing based spiritual transformation system is detrimental to the physical, psychological, and spiritual health of creative-emotional people.

- The historical background and the spiritual traditions that still use these methods today

- The four basic personalities that are encompassed within the creative-emotional personality category.

- Which Divine Energy fuels this inner transformation

- The natural progression of mystical transformation for a creative-emotional person

Let's take look back into history to see the development of the two Divine Energies.

SOLVING THE MYSTICAL PUZZLE

Throughout time, humans have been trying to untangle the mysterious puzzle of life. Those who could find the entrance into the mystical world of the gods received greater powers or ease of life. But, every time someone found a piece to the puzzle, they then had to find a way to pass on what they had discovered. Words didn't exist, or weren't available, to describe the discoveries. So, symbols had to be developed. The symbols that the ancients used to depict the divine came from the environment around them. Over time, a system of education arose to teach the deeper realities that lay beneath the surface of our everyday existence. We know this because archeology has documented flower-strewn burials, acoustically modified worship spaces, and cave paintings that incorporated aspects of the human combined with the divine that date back thousands of years. The ancients understood that the key to achieving enlightenment was to unlock the secrets of spiritual wisdom.

This spiritual wisdom did more than teach when the salmon returned or when to plant and harvest the grains. The spiritual experiences caused an inner change. It gave either an expansion of awareness that heightened the senses or it gave the mind the ability to use the imagination to plan and create. This wisdom was so beneficial to the welfare of the community that the elders passed down these skills to the children of the clan. The clues to inner transformation were encoded and placed into the sacred religious teachings of each culture and can still be found in the myths, art, symbols, and rituals handed down through time. They give us the procedures to change from an ordinary human being into one that can heal with a touch, hear through telepathy, or simply radiate loving vibes everywhere they go.

Those who discovered and utilized these clues were called mystics. A mystic believes that the temple of God is within each person. Instead of building a house or temple for God in the physical realm, the temple where God lives is built within the soul. This can only be achieved through direct personal contact with the essence of the divine. The inner being is transformed into an inner temple through the practices of the spiritual student. These methods bring about an *experience* or an *awareness* that changes the inner being from the inside, out.

When we look at the collection of ancient mystical writings we find that there are two very different methods for transforming the soul. The patriarchal cultures that worshiped the sun, such as the Romans, developed the esoteric path that killed the ego. The modern name for this method of mystical transformation is *The Hero's Journey*. The matriarchal spiritual schools revered the moon and developed the esoteric path of giving birth to the divine child. The modern name for this method of mystical transformation is *The Grail Path*.

The Grail Path and The Hero's Journey are diametrically opposite paths. The Grail Path utilizes The Divine Power of Grace to cleanse the inner being and grow the Divine Child. The Hero's Journey uses the Divine Power of Kundalini to initiate the inner transformation by killing the ego and heightening the senses. It does not matter if you call these twins Dark and Light, Bread and Wine, Yin and Yang, Lightning and Snake, or Adam and Eve. These mystical twins, through their metaphorical portrayals, show up throughout the ages and in a multitude of cultures.

We find a reference to the twin mystical paths in the earliest teaching of Christianity, *The Didache*. *Didache* is Greek and is translated as *Teaching*. *The Didache* is the oldest known lesson plan of Christian theology. It is purported that the original twelve apostles used *The Didache* to teach new converts to the Christian faith. The first line of *The Didache* reads:

There are two ways,

one of life and one of death,

and there is a great difference

between these two ways.

Via Appia was the name of the main road through Italy during the Roman Empire. In English, this name is translated as the Appian Way. Notice, it is not called the Appian Road. The many words used to denote a road in Latin are descriptive. They either describe the materials used to create the road or its functional use of movement or travel. So when this line states that there are *two ways*, it is saying that there are two different paths that can be traversed. This line is speaking of The Way of Life *and* the Way of Death. There are several Bible passages referring to these two *Ways* or spiritual paths. The Grail Path is the Way of Life, since it conceives and gives birth to the Divine Child. The Hero's Journey is the Way of Death, since its focus is to kill the ego.

Christian tradition honors The Grail Path with the celebration of Christmas. During the festival of Christmas, Christians celebrate the birth of the Divine Child to the Virgin Mary at the darkest part of the night, during the darkest time of the year. Midnight service on Christmas Eve is marked by an ambiance of soft light emanating from a multitude of candles. Some ceremonies include a candle lighting activity where a light is kindled from a central candle and passed to all members of the congregation creating a wave of illumination within the worship space. Since the invention of electricity, light is now available 24 hours a day, compromising the natural rhythms of nature. We, in the modern age, miss the significance of moving from the complete darkness of the outer world into the softly lit cavern of the inner being. Instead of seeing the Christmas story as the spiritual process of inner illumination for the creative or emotional person, we spin our intellectual wheels trying to scientifically prove how a virgin can conceive and give birth to a son without the help of a mate. Or worse. The beauty of the account is dismissed as a meaningless tale that is used to keep the masses happy and under control.

The Taoist tradition recognizes the reality of two distinct inner energies. The One Presence or the All in All produces two energies. In the Bible, the One God produces day and night. In Taoism, we find the Twin Energies of spiritual development referenced in the 42nd chapter of the *I Ching*, which reads:

The Tao produced The One,

The One produced The Two,

The Two produced The Three,

The Three produced ALL Things.

In the shortest creation story of any culture, the beginning of creation starts with the undifferentiated One. The One is a black *Nothingness* that is electrified with pure potential. Taoists do not use anthropomorphic symbols, like Father Sky or Mother Earth, to convey the divine principles. Taoist tradition is an energy-based philosophy. The Two that emerge from The One refer to the two energies of Yin and Yang. These two energies are not considered to be opposites. Neither is thought of in the dualistic way of good vs. bad. Yin and Yang are the foundations of a dynamic system that is in constant fluctuation and change. The Taoists realized that you couldn't have light without darkness. The dark letters on this page are visible because the background is white. If the letters were also white, then it would be impossible to read the writing.

The word "Tao" means road, path, or doctrine. It is usually thought of as *the flow of the universe*. To become one with the Tao means to harmonize one's will with the underlying natural order of the universe. The outcome of harmonizing one's will with the Tao leads to the "full coming into being" or enlightenment. *The Secret of the Golden Flower* is a classic Chinese spiritual manual that is used by the lay members of the Taoist spiritual community. The book's beautiful metaphorical language describes the energetic process of creating the Divine Child that is born in the lowest chamber of the soul. This is very similar to the Christmas story of Mary giving birth in a "stable," which was usually the basement level of the home where the animals were kept.

The Grail Path can also be found in Buddhism. The Buddha's flower sermon is the simplest form of Grail Path teachings. Legend states that one day the Buddha gathered all his disciples for a teaching. When everyone had gathered, the Buddha held up a single white lotus. He said nothing and looked around the room for any sign of acknowledgement or understanding. Mahakasyapa, who was considered the most stupid disciple by his contemporaries, then smiles. Mahakasyapa was then declared a holder of the Dharma and became the founder of the Buddhist School that is known as Zen today. Here we have the rare man who specialized in the Grail Path. Why did Mahakasyapa smile? What did he understand that none of the other disciples could decipher? The scholars have debated the meaning of this Zen styled koan throughout the ages. It will all become clear when we look deeply into the qualities and symbolism of the flower.

The medieval tales of Camelot depicted the Quest for the Holy Grail as a path for men who had achieved the supreme status of becoming a knight. In pre-historical and Biblical times, this path was traditionally reserved for priestesses and women. The symbols used in this path reflect the understandings and life processes of the average woman who moves from young virgin maiden, to bride, to mother, and finally to wise woman. In a culture that considers the death of the ego as the supreme way of inner spiritual transformation, The Grail Path has moved into obscurity and is nearly lost. There are few masters today who understand, much less specialize in, the process of bringing wholeness to the emotional or creative person.

It does not matter which spiritual path you choose. Wrestling with the monsters of the unconscious can be both dangerous and frightening. When we delve into the depths of the soul, we step into a shadowy world that can only be described in metaphorical terms. This is why the path of spiritual transformation is considered mysterious.

The mystery behind spiritual metaphor and

Esoteric practice is **ENERGY**.

Energy is invisible. We all know about the invisible energy called gravity. It is the force that pulls all matter down to the earth. Life on this planet lives, moves, and breathes within a gravitational field. Yet, it wasn't until the 1600's that gravity was discovered, described, and mathematically proven by Isaac Newton. Pre-scientific man had no direct language or mathematical skills to describe energy and how it flowed. That is why the ancients passed down the qualities of the two different energies and the processes of the two paths of inner spiritual transformation through the method of story.

It takes extensive practice or a special experience to comprehend the divine energies. Myth and parable provide the metaphorical vehicle needed to identify the divine energies and develop them to their highest potential. The identification process has three parts. First, the aspirant must feel or perceive the energy. Second, once the energy is properly identified in the soul, it can then be expanded and channeled through practices and rituals. Lastly, the knowledge is communicated to the next generation of adherents.

The Grail path is a mystical path. It is a quest of inner transformation for the creative or emotional person. The goal of the Grail Path is to fill the soul with the *Light* of the Divine Power of Grace. The process begins at the crown of the head. The first vision of the inner eye is of a shallow pool of light, which myth and legend equates to a platter. With continued practice, the light continues to flow and fill the crown chakra until it overflows into the chakra below. This process of filling each chakra and then flowing over into the chakra below continues until all seven chakras are opened and filled with light. As the light within increases, the platter expands to a cup and at its fullest point looks like a cauldron. When the inner being is totally filled, the light overflows into what is known as the aura. This is the origin of the glowing, egg-shaped halo that surrounds the entire body of the saints and the blessed ones.

You can find multiple depictions of this inner light in artworks and illuminated manuscripts. It is within this egg, also known as the Cosmic Egg, that the divine child is conceived and born.

The Holy Grail is not an object that can be found in the physical world. It resides within the psyche and can only be seen through the mind's eye or imagination. The mindset and practices of the seeker create the Holy Grail, The Cosmic Egg, and the Divine Child. During the entire transformation, the Kundalini does not rise through the base chakra, which means that Hieros Gamos *does not* take place. This is why the seeker of the grail is called a "Virgin" and why another name for this spiritual path is *The Virgin's Path*.

Now that we are aware that there are two distinct and opposite paths of attaining spiritual wholeness, it is **critical** that spiritual teachers understand the differences between the two spiritual paths of attainment. Most teachers are only aware of the path that they themselves traveled. They then set out to teach every spiritual student in their method and unwittingly harm the psyche of many of the students they guide. Knowing which path will best benefit the student is the key to the success or failure of the teacher.

A teacher is only qualified to teach the spiritual path they followed and accept only the students who will benefit by traveling that same spiritual path. Just as an English teacher is not qualified to teach math, a master of the Hero's Journey is not qualified to guide those who follow the Grail Path. While there are rare individuals who are dually qualified, most spiritual masters need to screen their students, accept only those who will benefit from their form of teaching, and refer everyone else to qualified teachers of the other path. So, let's review:

The Grail Path uses the Divine Power of Grace

to consolidate the undifferentiated feminine

psyche and bring forth the masculine principle

in the form of the Divine Child.

The Hero's Journey uses the Divine Power of
Kundalini to break through the blockages that
ego creates and expands the mind into the
Oneness of undifferentiated space.

It's time to turn our attention to the Grail Path. We will look into how to choose practices that will be beneficial to positive spiritual progress, the qualities and symbols of the Divine Power of Grace, the transformative process along the Grail Path, and finally the Men of the Grail.

CHOOSING SPIRITUAL PRACTICES

Each spiritual path employs a different divine power to fuel the inner transformation. The Divine Power of Grace is the downward, contracting force, while The Divine Power of Kundalini is the upward, expansive force. The goal of spiritual transformation is to fill the inner being with beneficially transforming divine energy. When the inner being is filled and the transformation is complete, the transforming divine energy opens the other end of the chamber. This allows the other divine energy to fill the emptied space. When you change paths, you are changing the divine power that is being put to use. Just as gravity and thrust cancel each other out, the same is true of Grace and Kundalini. It is like taking two steps forward, then two steps back. Forward progress toward enlightenment is impossible when the energies are continually flip-flopped.

Try this little thought exercise. Imagine a piece of paper hovering in midair. Place your finger on the underside of the paper. Now, thrust your finger upward. The paper moves upward. Remove you finger and use the other hand to represent gravity and push the paper downward. Again, it moves downward. Now, take both hands. Place one finger underneath the paper pushing up and the other finger on top of the paper pushing down. If both fingers use the same amount of force, the paper is stuck in the same place and does not move. If you switch back and forth between the energies, the paper just seesaws up and down never moving closer to any goal.

If you are working toward inner transformation,
it is important to choose a path and stick with it
until you have reached completion.

It must be understood that rituals and practices are the medicinal remedies for the ills of the spiritual body. Just as you would not walk into a pharmacy and gobble down any random pill you find there, it is not wise to take up any spiritual practice without knowing what spiritual ill it was designed to treat. It is also important to consider the interactions between practices. Many practices can cause great harm when they are mixed with practices from other religions. A person that experiences the emotions of others, who are emotionally based, or has an imaginative or creative mindset, will benefit by using the contracting and solidifying force of Grace. Grace creates a buffer from the emotional outpourings of others, calms the inner emotions, and confines the mind to the situation at hand.

The ancient masters kept the most potent practices secret. They transmitted the secret practices telepathically and verbally only to those students who were emotionally and morally ready to receive these teachings. This kept the mind-blowing effects of the advanced practices out of the hands of those who would use them for purposes of destruction and control. Unfortunately, the Internet has allowed the dissemination of these advanced practices to those who do not understand the dangers of what they are doing.

Ancient masters tested potential students and rejected those who would not benefit from their style of teaching. The masters were not elitists, nor were the rejected students spiritually incompetent. The masters knew that the remedies they employed would only work for student of a specific character. An aspirin will only help those with a headache. Heartaches need a different type of medicine.

We know that there are two spiritual paths. Each path uses one of the twin energies to fuel the inner transformation. Yet, there are multiple religions and they contain an untold number of practices and rituals. How do we know which religions or spiritual practices will be compatible with The Grail Path? It's not easy. Every major religion contains elements of both spiritual paths. The following are a few clues that can help with determining what energy is underlying the spiritual mechanics.

Beneficial Religions and Practices for the Creative and Emotional Person

- Roman Catholic

- Buddhist

- Tao

- Zen

- Islam

- Reiki Healing Techniques

- Mindfulness Meditation

- Internal Family Systems Psychological System

- Qi Gong – (spin the energies to the left as you practice)

- Tai Chi - (spin the energies to the left as you practice)

Here are some key phrases that will help you determine which religions and practices will be compatible with your spiritual development.

- Diversity is honored

- Lightwork or developing the Light Body

- Peace and Harmony are revered

Religions and Practices to Avoid for the Creative and Emotional Person

- Protestant

- Hindu/Yoga

- Freemasonry

- Alchemy

- Sufi

- Judaism/Kabbalah

- Transcendental Meditation

- Jungian Psychology

Here are some key phrases that will help you determine which religions and practices will cause setbacks in your spiritual development. *If you hear any of these phrases leave that person or spiritual group immediately!*

- Reverence for finding the Darkness, Void, or undifferentiated space as a final destination

- You must die before you die

- Ego must Die

- Kill the Flesh

- Any kind of Spiritual Warfare

  - Those who fight the devil are actually causing the Divine Power of Kundalini to rise within the spiritual system.

Please understand that these are general recommendations. We are all individuals that have unique needs. The practices that work for you may not work for someone else. *It is imperative to test each practice for a short time. Three days should be enough time to perceive the affects of a chosen practice.*

Keep a journal of your practices and evaluate each practice according to the emotions that are felt during the practice and the time following the practice. This is like keeping a food journal to determine if you have an allergy. **If you seem to have more anxiety, depression, brain fog, blackouts, or physical discomforts *especially while you are doing the practice*, stop that practice immediately!**

There will be times when buried issues arise that can cause unease. Practices should, for the most part, provide clarity and be pleasant. If it doesn't seem that anything is happening, keep doing the practice. Many times the effects of practice are subtle and it will take time to notice physical progress.

THE QUALITIES AND THEIR SYMBOLS

There are three characteristics that are exclusive to the Divine Power of Grace: Grace flows downward; Grace spins to the left; and Grace is calming, joyous and peaceful. The Divine Power of Grace is like a perfectly cut, glimmering jewel. Each facet represents a different stream of thought because the lens of cultural belief dictates spiritual metaphor. It does not matter which facet you view, each quality is a reflection of Grace. Interpretation can stem from any one of the facets or as a layering of multiple symbols.

Today we are at a crossroads of belief. For millennia, temples, churches and mosques have been the places for those who believe that God must be worshipped in a certain place, on a certain day. There have been many who follow the mystical path of inner transformation without needing to sit or kneel in a building while listening to a person of the cloth tell them what they should believe. There is a middle ground, however, where religious practices are used to build the inner temple while attending church and belonging to a religious community. No method of spiritual practice is better than another. Transformation can take place from either the outside, in or the inside, out. It is just a matter of personal preference.

THE FLOW OF GRACE

While there are many different viewpoints and interpretations of The Divine Power of Grace, there is one fact that the ancient cultures embraced. Grace flows downward. The downward motion of the Divine Power of Grace can be represented in many ways. Generally, the symbolic streams are defined as water, light, and fertility. Water was prized in all its forms. Lakes, springs, streams, rivers, rain, and snow were viewed as signs of Grace or the blessing of Father God. Other cultures valued light and the oils that help the light to shine as the highest attainment. To this day, Buddhism calls its highest attainment En*light*enment. Agrarian cultures focused on fertility. The dance between the masculine and feminine principles created the ultimate attainment, which were the procreation of animals and the harvest of vegetable foodstuffs. This evolved into an elaborate group of sacrificial symbols. The gifts of bread, rice, milk, and oil represented and esteemed The Divine Power of Grace.

Since this energy falls from the heavens above, the ancients considered Grace to be the essence of Father Sky. The elements that emanated from the sky like rain, snow, and lightening, are the most common metaphorical symbols used to represent The Divine Power of Grace. We find that rivers and waterfalls are considered masculine because water flows from high point to low point. When we go back in Christian history, before the era of Constantine, Grace was considered the masculine spiritual principle or The Divine Masculine. The indigenous peoples of the Americas also considered water and rivers to be male. In the song *Colors of the Wind,* from the Disney Movie *Pocahontas*, the rainstorm and the river are referred to as her brothers.

> Wrapping your mind around the idea that
>
> The Divine Power of Grace is a masculine
>
> principle is the first hurtle to understanding
>
> the spiritual metaphor of the first century.

When Constantine consolidated the Christian belief system, the polarities of the Divine Energies were flipped to synchronize the Christian ideals with the patriarchal Greco-Roman theology. In order to understand ancient texts that were written before the 4th century, we must go back to the earliest interpretations of the spiritual metaphors.

The ancients were superior observers. The celestial bodies and the night sky were intensely studied. The movements of the planets and stars marked the seasons and the cycles of life. The star, moon, moonlight, and moonbeams are yet more symbols that characterize The Divine Power of Grace. The silvery light of the moon and stars falls softly from an ebony sky. The night sky was a perfect metaphor for the beginning of the creative personality type's spiritual journey, which is the darkness of the undifferentiated cosmos. A woman's twenty-eight day menstrual cycle makes it easy to understand why the moon, which oscillates between light and dark in a twenty-eight day cycle, would be chosen to symbolize the filling and emptying of the womb. However, it was the depiction of a star, which was considered the Light of Heaven or Heavenly Light, that represents one who was filled to over flowing with light. While the average woman experiences the filling and emptying of the womb, the star was considered a high spiritual achievement because it would shine every night and does not experience darkness. In Egypt, the reappearance of the star Sirius marked the beginning of the flood season. The layering of the symbols, a river of water that is overflowing and a star whose light falls from a dark sky, doubles the impact of the meaning.

Finally, we come to the vegetative and foodstuff symbols. The ancients lived in a culture that viewed spiritual forces as gods and goddesses. When long-term observation revealed that rain makes crops grow, the ancients assumed that the essence of Father Sky was planting and watering seeds that then grew within Mother Earth. Flowers, Trees, and eventually crops were considered fruits of the womb of Mother Earth. It was believed that the sexual union between the forces of the Divine Masculine and Divine Feminine is what brings forth abundance. This type of sexual union is very different from the Hieros Gamos of The Hero's Journey. The insemination that takes place on The Grail Path comes from above, preserving the 'virginity' of the aspirant. The resulting conception takes place without the sin of sexual union and is, proverbially, immaculate.

White flowers, like the rose, the lotus, and the edelweiss, symbolized the Divine Power of Grace. These flowers provide a quadruple layering of symbolism. Metaphorical layering insured that the esoteric meaning would be transmitted. No matter how you interpreted the symbol, the derived esoteric meaning would be the same.

- These flowers are white, the color of purity and virginity.

- These flowers must be planted in the ground and then require the blessing of rain to bloom.

- These flowers are shaped like a cup or bowl.

- The reproductive process of flowers and flowering fruits does not require breaking through the bottom of the blossom.

- Insemination is a mysterious affair that takes place either on the wind or from insects that fly down from the sky. The fruit then develops and grows within the confines of the flower's petals.

Now, we can go back to the understanding of Mahakasyapa, the founder of Zen. It seems that he had contemplated the characteristics of a flower. He had considered the planting of the seeds, the watering of the seedling, and growth of the plant that could then flower. He had further pondered the insemination process, which did not break through the bottom of the blossom. Once inseminated, the fruit then develops within the boundaries of the flower's petals. The fruit's growth will eventually surpass the size of the flower. Only those who have experienced this inner spiritual process are able to recognize The Grail Path after a presentation of a flower.

The propagation and harvest of grains lead to the invention of bread. Bread was a staple in the diet of the ancients. The significance of bread can be illustrated by the fact that the Egyptian word, 'aish,' means both bread and life. In the Old Testament, Manna is described as a type of bread that falls from the sky. This is another prime example of metaphorical layering.

The colors that represent The Divine Power of Grace are the colors associated with its metaphorical symbols. Clear or crystalline comes from the water-based facet. The Light-based cluster gives us the colors of silver and iridescent. The vegetative or virginal cluster is symbolized by the color white.

THE EMOTIONAL QUALITIES OF GRACE

The Divine Energy of Grace is also associated with emotional properties. People with creative-emotional personalities live by their emotions. These people do not think - they feel. Feeling requires vibration. Just as our ears pick up the vibrations of sounds, emotional people pick up vibrations from the environment. Noise is not the only thing that sends out vibrations. My grandmother would refer to striking colors as being "loud." The ancients had a name for those who could feel deeply: "People who Hear." Today, through the efforts of scientists, we know that these people's brains favor the Imagination Network.

There are four characteristics that fall under the umbrella of those who prefer the Imagination Network. The creative personality is open to all possibilities. The emotional personality is caring. The empathic personality is sensitive to vibration. The imaginative personality can run simulations in the mind. Each of these gifts can be a great strength, or a huge detriment. So, the goal of spiritual practice for the creative-emotional is equanimity or emotional balance.

The creative personality is one that is open to all possibilities. Their minds reside in undifferentiated space. These people can bring together ideas and concepts from different fields to create solutions to problems. They can see the connections of a piece of furniture - the wood it was made from - the forest that the tree came from - the seed that was planted - and on and on. Mental focus is required to use the mind in this way. Getting wrapped up in the emotions of the problem prevents the mind from finding a solution. While their strength is to be out in open space, all creation takes place within the parameters of reality. Constraints such as cost, time, legalities, the principles of physics, and safety considerations are just a few of the realities that need to be incorporated into the design and implementation of any creative project. The untrained creative who does not understand the concept of parameters sits in an endless loop of new ideas or possibilities. This lovely space cadet has a hard time thinking linearly, being on time, or seeing a project to completion.

The emotional personality views life from a caring perspective. Giving or protecting can manifest as caring. Understanding the feelings of others and protecting them from harm is a necessary part of caring for infants, the sick, and the elderly. Sometimes the most caring thing to do is to give nothing so the person will be responsible for himself or herself. Nurses and physical therapists will tell you that half of their job is to make patients get out of bed and walk on their own. Caring can include the environment, animals, and the Earth itself. What happens when you care too much? Every disturbing news story upsets the emotional balance of an emotional person and lights the fire of anger or hopelessness. Every interaction becomes bogged down with emotional baggage. When the caregiver is over protective and takes care of every need, patients or children are not allowed to develop skills on their own. This also leads to what is known as mama bears or helicopter moms. These caregivers go above and beyond the basic protection of the weak and infirm. They harass college professors and employers, not understanding that they are contributing to their child's inability to function as an adult in the world.

Feeling can take the form of sense perception that originates outside one's self. An empath is one whose sensory perception is so acute that they can feel the slightest changes in the environment around them. They can feel the vibrations emanating from colors, people, animals, as well as sound. The empath is not creating the waves; the waves of noise and emotion are coming from the outer environment. Empaths will tell you that the vibrations of the world around them can be overwhelming. Something as simple as a color can be disturbing. An untrained empath finds it impossible to distinguish the difference between what vibrations are theirs and what vibrations are coming from the environment. The outer world is perceived as an active war zone that contains constant incoming bombardment.

The best way to describe the imagination is to relate it to a movie screen. The screen can run by itself, playing and replaying worries or emotional events or it can be trained to visualize plans and outcomes. The most extraordinary example of the ability to visualize comes from ancient Egypt. The ancient Egyptians did not draw architectural plans. A builder was trained to imagine the plans, down to the smallest detail, in his mind. One of the most famous Egyptian builders was Imhotep. He was the architect for King Djoser who designed and built the first step pyramid. Imhotep means "the one who comes in peace, is with peace." Due to his amazing accomplishments, Imhotep was one of the few commoners to be accorded divine status and worshipped as a god after his death. The imagination can also be used to visualize outcomes. Einstein used his mind to do what he called "thought experiments" to test his scientific theories. A simple thought experiment could be: Imagine two cogs, with the spokes enmeshed together. Now, imagine that one of the cogs is turned to the left. What happens to the other cog? Did you "see" the other cog turn to the right? Another facet of this skill is that the brain cannot tell the difference between what is imagined and what happened in reality. Athletes use this skill to practice their routines. It has been scientifically proven that mentally imagining a skill can be just as beneficial as physically practicing. What happens when this skill is untrained and allowed to run wild? We can imagine the most horrible fears to the point of incapacitation. We can literally worry ourselves sick.

The one thing that all these personality types have in common is the need to bring peace to the emotions and clarity to the mind. The creative needs to clarify parameters so decisions can be made and work can progress. The emotional types need to clarify the long-term consequences of their actions. The empath needs to clarify and strengthen their own vibrations so that they can turn off the vibrations of the environment at will. The imaginative type needs to discipline the mind to visualize only what is asked for and not random worries and fears. The Divine Power of Grace is the energy that clarifies the mind and calms the soul. It brings the Peace that passes all understanding.

The emotional transformation of the spirit is incorporated into the Christian liturgy during Advent, which takes place during the four weeks prior to Christmas. The word Advent is derived from the Latin word 'adventus,' which means "coming." Just as a pregnant woman must wait for the delivery of her child, Christians spend the weeks before Christmas in hopeful anticipation of the birth of the Divine Child. As more and more Grace is brought into the spiritual system, the emotions become more and more positive. The first quality the aspirant experiences is Hope. While complete mastery is a long way off, it becomes clear that there are methods and processes that can bring anxiety and mental fog to an end. The next emotional quality that is experienced is Love. This type of love is very different from the hot love of passion. It is a selfless love we give to friends or the love a parent gives to a child. Jesus called this type of love, "Agape." When the Love of the Father in Heaven is felt, a dawning of acceptance brings confidence to the psyche. When the Divine Power of Grace expands even further into the spiritual system, the aspirant feels the Joy of life. The joyousness of trees, animals, and even inanimate objects can be discerned. Final attainment is accompanied by the feeling of Peace. Worry is gone. Confusion is gone. Emotional turmoil is gone. The mind is crystal clear and operates as a servant to the needs of the moment.

The fruit of a spiritual master that specializes in The Grail Path is Hope, Love, Joy, and Peace. If you do not experience these joyous and calming emotions when you are around a proclaimed spiritual master, then either they do not specialize in the Grail Path or they are not masters at all.

29

The Four Noble Truths map out the basics of Buddhism. The First Noble Truth is that there is suffering. The Buddha was not talking about the outer circumstances of the world. The word the Buddha used was Dukkha. Dukkha can be translated as suffering, anxiety, or uneasiness. Dukkha can arise from union with that which is displeasing, separation from that which is pleasing, or not getting what you want. He is saying that when our minds and our emotions are out of control, we suffer. Believe it or not, it is possible to be in a terrible circumstance and not suffer if we have control of our minds and emotions. Jesus went through a horrible ordeal on the cross, but the only time he experienced emotional suffering is in the moment when he cries, "My God, My God, why have you forsaken me?" So, the first step to enlightenment is to recognize that our minds and emotions are running rampant. It is hard to realize that there is another way of being until you experience a moment of Peace. The Second Noble Truth states that *Desire* is the cause of suffering. Craving excitement, seeking delight, and clinging to what is pleasurable are the issues that must be faced. The Third Noble Truth tells us that by putting an end to the craving and clinging, the suffering, anxiety, and uneasiness will stop. The Fourth Noble Truth is the prescription to liberation. The basic practices to end suffering are behaving decently, cultivating discipline, and practicing mindfulness and meditation. In this way it is possible to end the emotional turmoil of Anger and Hatred and the resulting mental fog of Delusion.

The well known Buddhist monk, Thich nhat Hanh, teaches that when you recognize that your mind is sad to immediately think on the opposite emotion of happiness to bring balance to the emotions. If you are jealous, then think on gratitude and appreciate all the things you already have. Balancing the mind and the emotions is like training a puppy. You have to be ever vigilant and not allow it to go potty in the house. At first, accidents do happen. So, be compassionate with yourself. Gently bring the mind away from its worries or fears and begin again.

The Taoists believe that each person is responsible for the emotions that arise within. Life's outer circumstances will present trying times that overload the spiritual system with either Yin or Yang. It is possible to transform the negative emotions into a positive life force by concentrating on the opposite emotion or energy. It is also possible to exchange the internal energy of the body with external energy of the universe. The Taoists believe that each organ and muscle has the potential to trap negative emotions. Expelling or suppressing unwanted or negative emotions drains us of life-force energy. The better way of dealing with emotions is to balance the organs through meditation or sound therapy.

The most basic negative emotions are fear, anger, and hopelessness. If these emotions are allowed to run rampant they become habitual. The first step toward balancing the emotions is to recognize the habit and then reprogram the mind to a new response. Once we have control over our emotions, it is possible to view life from a state of non-attachment. Instead of being dragged into a swirling drama of emotions, we can see the patterns that constantly repeat themselves. From this higher perspective, we can learn the life lesson and change the direction of our lives. The main goal of Taoist meditation is to create, transform, and circulate the positive internal energy. The principle that Qi follows Yi means that where the intention goes the energy follows. Once the meditator has control of the internal energy, it can be applied to promoting mental and physical health, creative and inventive endeavors, or nurturing the spiritual embryo of immortality.

THE SECRET OF REFILLING GRACE QUICKLY

In the pandemonium of life, we do not have the luxury of waiting until the mind calms down to experience clarity. The Buddhist precept of "not stirring the water" is not relevant. Living in the world stirs the water. Traffic, a flat tire, the boss wants a report on a turn of a dime, and a misunderstanding are all things that "stir the water." Rebalancing is a constant activity. We who live in the world don't have the luxury to sit in a cave for years waiting for the mind to clear. How do you find clarity and emotional balance in a world that does not stop?

The secret is that Grace spins to the LEFT.

We do not have to stop the world in order for balance to occur. As the masters of many religions have said, balance takes place when we

31

consciously spin the energy in the opposite direction of the disturbance. This does not mean running away from everything that is upsetting. It means that we must be conscious of the energies, as they are moving through our bodies. It is easier to move energy through the body when it is put into motion first. This can be done in two different ways. You can physically spin your body, like the whirling dervishes. Once the body stops, the energy continues to spin through the spiritual system. It's like when you spin a can with a ball inside. Once the can stops, the ball continues to spin in the can. The other way is to envision that the pool of energy above the head is spinning to the left. As it spins, it will push the energy down through the system faster and shortening the time it takes to bring the spiritual system back into balance.

The Grail Path is sometimes referred to as The Left Hand Path because The Divine Power of Grace spins to the left. The Left Hand path is considered the wrong way by many cultures and religions. It is important to understand that that is true for those who believe that everyone has an ego that must die. When both of the Divine Energies are honored then there is no wrong path. The wrong path is the path that is wrong for you. If you are an emotional or creative personality who's brain runs on the Imagination Network, the Left-Hand Path is the most beneficial spiritual path for you.

The Celtic culture used the swirl to represent the direction of movement for the energies. If you trace the lines with your finger, you will notice that the patterns will either move to the left or in a counter-clockwise direction or to the right or in a clockwise direction. The swirl that spins to the left represented the energy that falls from the Sky. The swirl that spins to the right represented the energy that rises up from the Earth.

The Hindu culture also uses symbolism that represents the motion of the energies. First we have to understand how motion is depicted in simple drawings. The simplest drawings of the modern age are cartoons. The artist can infer motion to a stick character by adding lines behind the character. This simple drawing technique was used to create the swastika. The swastika is a cross or wheel in motion. How do

32

we know this? We can to do an experiment to understand what is being communicated. You can do the experiment in the physical realm or as a mind experiment. Begin with a cross. You can lash two pencils together or just imagine a solid cross. Next, tie ribbons or string to the ends of the four outer points. Now, spin the cross in either direction. Notice that the ribbons follow behind. If you spin the pencils the other direction, again the ribbons will change to follow behind. So, if the dashes on the points of the cross are on the right side, then the movement of the cross is to the left or counter-clockwise. If the dashes on the tips of the cross are on the left side, then the movement of the cross is to the right or in the clockwise direction.

CONNECTING THE CIRCUIT

The last stream of thought connects the circuit between the two energies. Just as Day brings Night and Yin brings forth Yang, Grace initiates Kundalini. The Law of Correspondence tells us that what happens in the outer physical world must also occur within the spiritual system. The ancients observed that when lightening struck the ground it started fires. Lightening coming down from the Sky initiates Fire that rises up from the Earth. As we have seen, lightening is not the only symbol used to represent Grace.

The oils that lit the lamps in ancient times were made from olives, grape seeds, and almonds. They are a fruit of the earth that had special qualities. These oils when poured into a lamp could produce fire and light. The ceremony of pouring oil on a person or anointing them with oil became part of the ordination of a priest, prophet or king and the consecration of venerated items. Anointed persons and objects became "most holy" because they now had the essence of The Father that brought forth the spiritual essences of Fire and Light.

There are several different stories in the Bible that connect the circuit between the two divine energies. In the story of Elijah in the book of 1st Kings, Elijah has proposed a contest between the different deities, Baal vs. Yahweh. Here the two systems of belief are pitted against each other. The contest consists of getting God to light the sacrificial fire. The Priests of Baal are practitioners of Kundalini. They try to start the fire by exciting the fire within through ecstasy, frenzy and blood letting. But, the fire on the alter does not light. Elijah is teaching that the opposite principle of Grace, which is represented by the water he pours on the fire, must be activated first in order for the fire to light. This Bible story is a tale of pure alchemy. In order to understand that this is a recipe of spiritual transformation, a complete understanding of the ingredients and their properties is needed. Water is a visual representation of the essence or energy of Father Sky. Water is cool and clear. Water pours downward. The water then spontaneously bursts into flames. Fire is a visual representation of the essence or energy of Mother Earth. Fire is red and hot. Fire shoots upward.

The story of Noah is another tale of that which falls raises you up. The essence of the story is that the rain falls from the sky and makes Noah's boat rise to the top of Mount Ararat. Noah did not climb the mountain. He floated to the top of the mountain on the water that poured from the sky. The Sumerian story of Gilgamesh also incorporated the flood story into its literature. So, the flood is a symbolic representation of an inner spiritual event that leads to inner transformation. Water that pours from the sky is the force that raises the boat of Noah to the top of the mountain.

The same teaching happens in the story of Jesus' Wedding. Jesus fills the earthenware jugs with water and it miraculously turns into wine. Let's blatantly point out the symbols.

- Earthenware Jars – Mankind was created from the dirt. So, we are talking about something going on within the body.

- Water is poured in first – Water is the physical representation of the essence of Father Sky. It is poured into the jar from the top.

- Water miraculously turns to Wine – A hole is not drilled into the bottom of the jar. Fire is not placed under the jar. Yet, the essence of Mother Earth, red wine, magically appears.

Evidence for the belief of connecting the circuit can be found in the burial rituals of each culture. Cultures that believe that people arose from the earth usually then bury the dead in the ground. This connects the circuit and returns the soul to the divine. Cultures that believe that people come from the heavens cremate the body. Tibetan Buddhists are known to perform what is known as "sky burials."

THE TRANSFORMATIVE PROCESS

The creative mind is celebrated for its undifferentiated nature. The lack of segregation or proverbial file drawers allows the creative personality to make connections between subjects that would not normally be put together. The downside of such an open nature can be overwhelm and emotional turmoil. Without the masculine principles of order, discipline, and integrity, the creative personality type has a hard time functioning in the real world. The creative personality tends to jump from one idea to another. They often sit in a state of confusion due to the inability to chop large projects into smaller, easily accomplished pieces. Defining priorities, adhering to budgets, meeting deadlines, following rules, or explaining their ideas in a logical manner are disciplines that require work and practice for the creative personality type to master. Those with a highly sensitive or empathic emotional nature feel bombarded by the waves of feeling and sound that emanate through normal life. Walking through busy streets, attending large gatherings, even making a simple trip to the store is an overwhelming and exhausting experience.

Once trained, the creative personality can become a genius. They seem to have a direct pipeline into the depths of reality. The mystery of the collective unconscious, including its archetypical world, opens to them. They can reach in at will and pull out the perfect design or solution. Writing, music, and dance flow from a seemingly divine source. The empath is no longer at the mercy of every sound or emotional outburst within his or her vicinity. They have gained the ability to selectively receive relevant information, while allowing the irrelevant to be sloughed off. The deeply observant nature of the creative personality bestows the ability to avoid the common hazards of life. They are able to see patterns and long-term consequences, which makes it possible to intuit solutions before a major crisis can explode. So, lets delve into the ancient process that turns a compassionate, creative bundle of confusion into a strategic laser mind.

The Chinese are famous for their knowledge of healing energies. Acupuncture and Acupressure are used to move the energy of the body, known as chi, through energy channels. Just like the blood and blood vessels of the body, the energy and the energy channels nourish the body with fresh energy and take away the harmful energies and waste products. It is thought that if there is a blockage in the energy flow then illness and disease will develop in that part of the body. These practices are much older than previously thought. The iceman, named Otzi, found in the Otzal Alps, had been preserved in a glacier for 5,300 years. He had tattoos on his body that identified the acupuncture points that would relieve his back and abdominal pain. This is an amazing find for two reasons: First, he was found in Western Europe. That is a long way away from central China where it was thought acupuncture was originally discovered and developed. The second reason this find was amazing is because Otzi's tattoos predate the recorded use of acupuncture in China by 2,000 years. We now know that the knowledge of internal energies is quite old and widespread, which is why much of the sacred literature throughout the world contains references to these energies.

The energies that are used for healing the body can also be used to heal the soul and develop the divine child. Just as the universe has a structure that is governed by invisible forces, so too does the inner being. We all know that electricity requires wires and circuit boxes to operate properly. The same is true for the invisible forces of Grace and Kundalini. The Grail Path is one of a pair of interlocking systems of energy transformation. We will be using the most basic of the ancient energy systems to transform the inner being into a temple where God lives. The energy that powers the inner transformation along The Grail Path is the energy that falls from the sky, what Christian theology refers to as Grace.

The inner being acts as the circuit box for the Divine Energies. The structure of the inner being contains a main energy channel, called the *axis mundi* that runs vertically through the center of the body. On this main channel are the seven chakras, or places of energy convergence. Each chakra acts like a fuse within the circuit box governing a specific area of the body. Each chakra also deals with a different aspect of personal development. Damage or blockages in a chakra, or in the region of a chakra, can create psychological issues as well as physical illness. The last elements of the inner structure are the two separate channels that stream the two divine energies of Grace and Kundalini. These two channels make concentric coils, connecting each chakra to the chakra above and below it. The channel for Grace twists to the left, while the channel for Kundalini twists to the right. The chakras are fed through these two conduits of energy throughout life. We see this represented in the two "snakes" wrapped around a central pole of the caduceus, which most recognize as the symbol for health and the medical profession, today.

A tenant in the Taoist tradition states that Qi follows Yi. This phrase is translated as, "energy follows thought." So, the idea that thought creates your reality is not just some whacky New Age idea. This is a tenant of Taoist spiritual life that is over 5,000 years old. The Taoist spiritual masters knew that if you do not have control of your thoughts, then you do not have control of the divine energies. Life events, beliefs, and emotions randomly move the two divine energies of Grace and Kundalini haphazardly through the system. The average person experiences ceaseless energy fluctuations that create physical and psychological highs and lows. These unbridled changes in body, mind, and mood can feel like a form of demon possession that drives a person to actions and substances in order to stop the constant vacillations.

True balance of the energy system requires that you take conscious control of the energies. The main energy channel remains closed until it is opened by a spiritual master or through extended energy practice. The mystical transformation begins when the *axis mundi*, or main energy channel, is opened. Once the main channel is open, then it becomes possible to direct the energies. While it is possible to open the main energy channel from either end, the *axis mundi* should **NEVER** be opened from both ends at the same time. We have discussed the horrific consequences and the shattering effects that the rise of Kundalini can cause in a virginal spiritual system in the opening chapter.

Below is a model of the inner transformational system. It includes the white masculine sphere interlocked with the red feminine sphere. Notice how the chakras along the axis mundi are enclosed within the almond-shaped intersection of the masculine and feminine. One side of the almond-shaped enclosure is red while the other is white. Notice how both Divine Energies are kept out of the inner system by a gate.

The Grail Path opens the *axis mundi* at the crown of the head to facilitate the downward flow of the Divine Power of Grace into the spiritual system. As the process continues through the system, the "platter" of Grace that was pooled in the heavenly realms transforms into a "cup" and eventually into a "bowl" or "cauldron." As we said before, each person is born, or develops in early life, an abundance of one or the other divine energy. The creative-emotional personality is born with or has accumulated an over abundance of Kundalini through their life experiences. Opening the upper gate allows The Divine Power of Grace to flow into the spiritual system and balance the existing surplus of Kundalini that has accumulated in the body.

THE MAIN SPIRITUAL PRACTICES OF THE GRAIL PATH

The Grail Path's mystical transformation is brought about by a combination of breath, meditation, and visualization. Conscious breathing means that we stop for a moment and concentrate our attention on the breath. We take our deepest breaths using the diaphragm. When done properly, the belly should expand to fill the lungs. For a greater impact, try sucking the belly in as far as it will go during exhalation. This will allow more air to flood into the body with each inhale. When you use conscious breathing as part of The Grail Path's spiritual practice, it is best to breathe in through the nose and out through the mouth. It pushes the energy down, causing it to pool and cleanse each chakra as it descends deeper into the spiritual system. This simple method of breathing is calming to the emotions and can be done anywhere. Train yourself to breathe consciously several times during the day. You can practice conscious breathing while standing in line at the grocery store, while waiting for the microwave to ding, while waiting for the traffic light to turn green, or at the top of the hour while at work. To add a kick to this practice imagine the energy above your head spinning to the left as you breathe in, then force the energy downward as you breathe out through the mouth. This little ½ Minute Meditation can keep your mystical transformation humming through the day and between major practice times.

Meditation is an important spiritual practice for mystical transformation. Spending time training the brain is absolutely necessary. The mind has a tendency to behave like a puppy. It needs constant supervision to keep it from chewing on unnecessary thoughts or pottying in the house. A fun but effective way to discipline the mind is to visualize your happy place. This place is not outside of you. Do not use this to escape the turmoil of your inner being. *This is your temple within.* You are building an atmosphere within your being that can be called upon at any moment. It can be used to remind you of the peace that dwells within, to calm yourself down during distressful events, or just to glow through your day. Begin by visualizing a place that is safe, beautiful, and peaceful. It can be a forest, a beach, a starry night, or any other place that suits your fancy. Name this place and use this name every time you open and close this meditation. Spend 5 minutes each day visualizing this place. If your mind wanders, gently bring it back without comment or punishment. As the days go by, add more sensory details like birdcalls, the aroma of the seaside, or the sensations of the wind blowing. When you close the meditation, thank this place by name and exit gently back into the physical world.

Another type of meditation is a lightwork meditation. We will be watching the process of the light as it flows into and through the spiritual system, which is why this type of visualization is called a process style meditation. Begin by settling into a meditative state with a few conscious breaths. Once you have become settled, visualize a star or pool of light above your head. Allow the light to stream down to the top of your head. We will now follow this meditation through the attainments.

FIRST ATTAINMENT - THE WEDDING OR LIFTING OF THE VEIL

The mystical ceremony that opens the gate at the top of the Axis Mundi has traditionally been called *The Wedding* or *The Lifting of the Veil*. The reasoning behind this metaphor is that the aspirant is now directly connected to Father Sky in order to receive *His* essence, The Divine Power of Grace. Michelangelo demonstrated the two different paths when he painted Adam and Eve on the ceiling of the Sistine Chapel. Adam is depicted as reaching up to God, while Eve is depicted as enfolded under the left arm of God. In ancient times, the placement of the wife was always on the left side of the man who was her husband. The symbolism that the "God" figure is naked to the waist provides two different clues to the path that was traditionally for women. First, it points to the fact that the woman on the left is His "wife," a person who is bound by a covenant or agreement. Secondly, since the genitals of God are covered, it shows that the "wife" is not the sexual consort. It is a paradox. While the aspirant is "married" to the Godhead, the "husband" is more like a father figure providing strength and protection. Today, as in ancient times, marriage is a legal contract. Both the bride and the groom make vows to a committed relationship that supersedes all physical conditions like sickness and health. This analogy is still used today when the Christian church is referred to as the bride.

When the crown chakra is opened, the veil of separateness is lifted. The concept of lifting a veil is another reason why the ancients used the marriage ceremony as a metaphor for this spiritual attainment. The

Oneness, the fact that all things are connected within the wholeness of being, is comprehended. Spiritual traditions throughout time acknowledge this Oneness. The Buddhists call it *the Void or Nothingness.* The Hindus separate this Oneness into two different types, the Unknowable - *Parabrahman* - and the Knowable - *Brahman.* Christians call this the One Power, One Presence, God Almighty. Taoists call the Oneness, The Tao. The Islamist doctrine of *Tawhid* holds that God is One and Single.

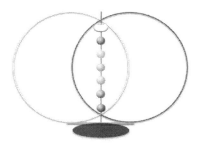

Supplemental First Attainment Practices

1. You can augment the basic lightwork meditation of this chakra by imagining the color purple, by chanting the mantra "Om" or "Ah," or by using the imagination to spin the energy within the crown chakra to the left.

2. Another practice during this phase of spiritual development is to contemplate the interconnectedness of all life. There is *nothing* in this world that stands alone. Everything that has manifested into this reality relies upon the interplay of innumerable factors to come into existence. Something as simple as the contemplation of a wooden chair can take many sessions and even years. The student is guided to contemplate the workmanship of the chair. This leads to contemplating the craftsman's training, the incidents and actions that lead to him or her deciding to be a craftsman, all the way back to key events in his or her childhood. If the chair was made in a

factory, contemplation of all the innovations and those who invented the machines that cut, shape, and assemble the wood into furniture is considered. The organization of a society that comes together and works at different jobs is another facet that allows a chair to be produced. Now, we get to the tree itself. Where the wood came from, its life in the forest, and its sacrifice to become shaped into a purpose can become a stream of contemplation. Finally, we come to the seed of the tree. The one in a million chance that it fell in a place where it could receive the needed nutrients to sprout and grow into a full size tree that could be used. These types of contemplations demonstrate the interconnectedness, complexity, and synchronicity of life and bring the student to awe and wonder.

3. The contemplation of the wooden chair prepares you for reviewing the aspects of your own life. Spiritual awakening is a process of accessing buried memories, understanding the situations and circumstances around key events, and realizing the wonder of how those things, many of them traumatic, made you into the unique and beautiful person you are today.

SECOND ATTAINMENT - OPENING THE THIRD EYE

As we continue the lightwork meditation, the Light of Grace flows downward. The chakra known as the third eye is opened and cleansed. This is the center of the imagination. Grace gives the ability to see patterns in nature, replay the situations and consequences of life, as well as gives the ability to see energy flows within ourselves. This is not the psychic ability that sees into the future per se. Seeing auras, looking into someone else's past, and seeing the future are the skills bestowed by the Divine Power of Kundalini. The activities of the Divine Power of Grace are limited to our own inner world.

Albert Einstein called the ability to use the imagination to play out consequences, "mind experiments." He had honed his mind to such a clear state that he could mentally picture the processes and outcomes of his mathematical equations. These visualizations gave Einstein the simple method for proving his $E=MC^2$ theory. Interior designers can envision a finished room from little pieces of paint, fabric, and wood on a design board. Corporate strategies require the ability to think backwards from an outcome in order to generate a timeline of actions. Imagining how people or vehicles will move through streets, venues, or events efficiently without conflict or confusion is a process-oriented skill. As you can see, this skill has applications and uses other than creating fantasy.

I had the pleasure of watching someone use their ability to visualize the process of how electricity flowed through electrical wires

45

during a home construction project. After upgrading the circuit box in my home, many rooms were not receiving power properly. Some outlets were sparking and others did not get enough power. The master electrician, who was sent to fix this wiring problem, stood in the center of my basement for 10 minutes visualizing how the electricity was running through my house. I watched in awe, as his eyeballs rolled around in his head, as he systematically followed the path of the electricity through the wiring. All the while, asking questions about which outlets were sparking and which were not getting enough power. He then told me that he was looking for a neutral wire that should be running from a specific junction to the circuit box. The neutral wire was attached to the junction he specified, but did not terminate in the circuit box. Sure enough, that main neutral wire had fallen down behind the drywall and was missed during the installation. Within 20 minutes he had diagnosed the problem, wired up the forgotten wire, and restored safe power to my whole house. The ability of visualization allowed the master electrician to fix a problem in minutes. It would have taken a lesser-experienced electrician hours of running through the house, opening multiple outlets, and testing the electrical flow with his instruments to get the same job done. Once you achieve a level of skill envisioning systems at work, then all systems are open to you. The third eye is not just the seat of design, strategy, and system processes, but also of Karma.

The Hindu belief system states that Karma is the backlash of events that you put into motion. If you steal, then your freedom will be taken away. If you are generous, then others will be generous to you. Understanding the outcome of your actions *before* you do them is key to keeping negative karma at bay. If you can behave in such a way that does not create a backlash, then your actions will not come back to haunt you. Imagine waves emanating from a rock that you just dropped into a pond. These waves will continue to expand out until they hit the shore. The waves will then bounce off the shore and move back to the location where the rock was tossed. If the action of the rock was negative, then the returning waves will also be negative. If the action of the rock was positive, then the returning waves will be positive.

The Taoist concept of Wu Wei – without action - and its companion concept of Wei wu Wei – action without action - has tentacles in the imagination center. This concept speaks of operating within the harmony of nature so that there is no reaction that comes from your actions. Knowing and understanding the natural processes of the universe allows one to act without disrupting the natural balances that are both within and without.

The Taoist energy system contains three focal points called tan t'iens. The tan t'ien is loosely described as an "elixir field" or "energy center." The Third Eye is the location of the upper tan t'ien. It is interesting to note that the average first century house in the Middle East contained three levels. The basement level was used as a place to stable animals. The main level was where the majority of the household business took place. The upper room, which was open to the sky, was where the family slept in the warmer months and where feasts took place. So, we could say that the Taoist upper tan t'ien is metaphorically equivalent to the Christian upper room.

Supplemental Second Attainment Practices

1. Practices that are designed to encourage and enhance the abilities associated with the imagination center are called visualizations. Visualizations are not just fluffy practices. Visualizations develop mental discipline because they require the mind to stay on task. Energy transformation visualizations, like the lightwork visualization we are following now, are process-oriented visualization practices. The seemingly simple visualization of light flowing through the body can be quite powerful. The addition of sound, color, and sensations can enhance the experience and engrain the energy movement through the pathways.

2. You can supplement the basic lightwork meditation of this chakra by imagining the color indigo, chanting the mantra "Om," or spinning the energy within the third eye chakra to the left.

3. Another type of visualization practice that boosts the ability of the third eye is what I call the "IF – THEN" practice. The practice begins with an action or current reality. The imagination is then used to intuit the resulting action or consequence. The possibilities for this practice can be endless. Imagining outcomes is a great game to play with children. Here are a few examples of IF – THEN visualizations.

    a. IF there are two interlinked cogs and I turn one of them clockwise, THEN which way will the other cog turn?

    b. IF I knit these two colors together, what will the sweater look like when I am finished?

    c. IF I hit my neighbor, THEN what do you think will happen?

    d. IF I spend all my money now on pleasant things, THEN what will happen if I lose my job? How will I survive when I am too old to work?

4. Visualizing timelines can greatly expand your mind's strategic ability. Begin by listing the final outcome, complete with a deadline date. It can be anything from an academic paper to an event like a wedding day. Once the final date is established, chop the project into smaller pieces. You will notice that some action items have prerequisites. For example, you won't be able to write the outline until the research is complete. Once the order is established, move backwards from the final deadline adding mini deadlines for research, outlining, and the average time it takes for an outside editor to go over your work. It might take the editor only a couple of hours to edit your work, but if he or she has an average of eight projects ahead of yours, then that extra time needs to be incorporated into your strategy. Otherwise, your paper will miss the deadline because it was sitting on the editor's desk. You can do

the same with anything from a dinner party to a work related project.

5. The use of archetypes as part of the visualization practice is widespread. The Tibetan Buddhists use both the positive and negative archetypes of their deities in their visualizations. Buddha and Tara are the most common deities used, but they are just the tip of the iceberg. The Catholic tradition has innumerable saints to contemplate. The Hindu religion have Shiva and Kali along with its many other gods and goddesses. Visualizing the Archangels is quite popular. A simple archetypal contemplation would be to use the Archangel Michael. Michael, the archangel of white light, is commonly depicted sitting on top of a red serpent or red dragon with his silver sword posed downward, ready to strike off the demon's head.

   a. It is important to note that these visualizations need to be understood as being inside you. The archetypes are aspects of you and are part of your personality. Imagine the images of the selected archetype inside your inner temple. When you keep the archetype within yourself, the energies within are beneficially activated.

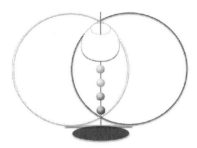

THIRD ATTAINMENT – THE OPENING OF THE MOUTH

As we continue this lightwork meditation, the image of the inner being becomes more and more like a cup. As the Divine Energy of Grace flows downward, it pours into the throat chakra. The throat chakra has many aspects because it governs both the mouth and the ear. The mouth is the place of creating sound. Intoning chants, singing, and prayers enhance the positive vibrations, while confessions unburden the soul of the negative aspects. Both are part of the mystical experience. Speaking sacred words and syllables is a common ritual practice. The simple blessing of food, or the saying of Grace, is an ancient spiritual ritual. Many ritual texts, like the Jewish Torah, require the intoning of the words, by a holy and trained professional scribe, as they are written. This is one of the many requirements that determine whether the document is holy. It is thought that the vibrations from prayers also sanctify both the ritual spaces and the worshipers. That is why many faiths require that ritual or ceremony be performed in a set space, on a regular basis. Just as the tone of a tuning fork will fade if it is not continually played, so too does the holiness of the space fade over time when ritual or ceremony ceases.

The ear is the instrument that receives vibrations. When this chakra is opened and functioning properly, then the blessings that are intoned by instruments or spiritual masters can be received and incorporated into the inner being. It is through this chakra that we can *feel* the ambiance of a ritual, a space, or a holy person. The ancients called people who used their ears as the primary source of information gathering, "Those who Hear." In the Book of Luke, the announcement of Jesus' birth to the shepherds was through the voices of the angels.

This chakra is an exchange valve. It can both send and receive vibrations. In the Book of Genesis, God breathes the breath of life into the mouth of the clay form of Adam. The early Christian practice of the spiritual kiss, discussed in the Gnostic Gospel of Phillip, is most probably based on this scripture. It describes that the way for the spiritual master to impart spiritual energies to disciples or spiritual students is through a kiss. When the Divine Energy of Grace reaches the throat chakra, it feels like a kiss on the mouth. The bridal kiss, or the Kiss of God, was considered a sign of this spiritual attainment.

A world event that exemplifies the power of the kiss happened on April 29, 2011. Who was not anxiously waiting for that special moment when newly married royal couple of William and Catherine kissed on the balcony? The exchange of energy can be just as magical for those who are watching as for those who are participating. That is because the vibrations from that exchange emanate through space. The reason the televised audience experienced the same excitement is because our imagination can replicate that sensation within ourselves even though we are not participating in the physical act of kissing.

The Breath of Life, which is similar to the Bible story when God breathes into Adam, was also very important to the ancient Egyptians. It was most commonly depicted in tombs as part of the funerary rituals performed on mummies to bring them back to life. The next king performed the ritual because he was now considered the highest male deity on earth. Only his essence contained the Grace needed to reanimate the inanimate mummy. The Opening of the Mouth Ceremony was also performed on statues and temple relief images so that they would become alive and undertake their spiritual functions.

The Buddhist eight fold path includes "Right Speech." Here we get into not just the morality and integrity of lying but also the realization of who we are. Those little tell tale Freudian slip-ups are barometers of the soul.

51

That which you speak of, is what you are.

That which comes out of your mouth has very little to do with the outer world. It is all about your inner world and your life experience. The issues and congealed thought patterns that harbor in your mind will spill out into both the words you say and the inner chatter that runs through your mind. The inner mind chatter becomes noticeable when life is quiet. Meditators comment that they never noticed how active the mind was until they started meditating.

The flip side of this realization is that this truth is the same for everyone. That which comes out of someone else's mouth, most likely, has nothing to do with you. They are speaking from their own inner world. This is the basis of the psychological concepts of perception and mirroring. A person will see and criticize in others what needs to be healed within themselves. This reminds me of an incident on a grade school playground. A bully had just hurled a nasty comment at his intended victim but instead of being offended and dragged into a fight, the child replied:

"I'm rubber and you're glue.

Everything you say,

bounces off of me

and sticks to you!"

Such a profound statement out the mouth of a babe!

Supplemental Throat Chakra Practices

1. You can supplement the basic lightwork meditation of this chakra by imagining the color Light Blue, chanting the mantra "Ham," or spinning the energy within the throat chakra to the left.

2. The spiritual practice that helps clear the throat chakra is to monitor what you say out loud. Keeping a log of your

conversations, and then reflect upon why you said that and where it came from, gives tremendous insight as to what needs to be healed within your psyche. If you are constantly making negative comments about dogs, then it is time to look into your experiences and find why. Did a dog bite you? Did a household pet create negative situations in your childhood? It is time to bring up these buried memories and open them to the wider situations and circumstances. This is a way to defuse them. It could have been that the dog that bit you had come from an abusive home and misinterpreted your raised hand as further abuse instead of a pat of love.

3. There are a couple of meditation practices that can help a person to survive the constant bombardment of mental chatter. The first is to notice each thought and label it as positive, negative, or neutral, then let it go. Another is to retrain the mind by reciting positive affirmations or using visualizations that infuse positive emotions.

4. The other meditation practice that can help with inner chatter is to choose a thought or an event that keeps popping up and then delve into the depths of its origins. Who said that to you? Why would anyone say such a thing? Once you widen the perspective of the situation, you will realize that that comment or event had nothing to do with you. It had everything to do with the inner nature of the person who said that.

5. Notice that we are using the wider perspective of the crown chakra, the viewing ability of the third eye, and the hearing ability of the throat chakra to navigate mental chatter. The abilities of the chakras are interrelated. As the skills and abilities of each chakra are honed and purified, the ability to negotiate the depths of the psyche increases. Answers as to why you do things the way you do come quicker and are dispersed easier. However, complex understandings can have

53

many facets. So, don't be surprised if an issue you thought was taken care of resurfaces. It just means that there is another side to the issue that needs to be resolved. The mystics speak of a winding staircase system of attainment. We circle around to the same event but we are now seeing it from a deeper level.

FOURTH ATTAINMENT – OPENING THE HEART

As the light of the Divine Power of Grace flows into the heart chakra, we enter the world of relationships. Love and how we relate to others are the functions of the heart chakra. The heart is the crossroads of all the energy channels. Once the heart is opened and is functioning properly it has the ability to transmute or chemically change negative emotion into positive, happy energy. The heart chakra has an enormous job. Scientists have found that the electromagnetic field generated by the heart is larger than the brain's electromagnetic field.

Compassion consists of giving Light, Grace and Encouragement, not pouring more sorrow or drama into the situation. *This attainment can require a lifetime of repeated lessons!* The first person we have to establish a positive loving relationship with is ourselves. We have begun to see and hear the murmurings of the inner self through the previous chakras. When we combine the ability of the crown chakra to open to the oneness of creation with the love of the heart chakra, we can love ourselves as the unique and amazing people we are in this moment. An open heart chakra allows us to bless misfortunes and forgive the missteps that have shaped us. This attainment challenges us to find the unlimited capacity to see the good in all things and to love, regardless of situation or circumstance.

Since the third eye chakra allows us to see the consequences of actions, love takes the form of what is needed in that moment. A baby needs a very different form of love than a young adult. Babies need to be completely protected and every need provided by a caregiver. A young adult needs to stand up for himself or herself, rely upon their own resources, and accept the consequences of their actions. Just as too much water will damage a plant, over protection will do long-term damage to the psyche of a child.

The same is true of all aspects in life. We can love our homes by keeping them clean and repaired. We can love our clothes by folding them nicely or hanging them in a closet. Friends who are moving will appreciate the help. We realize that it is not loving to feed a pet that extra scoop of food or too many snacks. While they may enjoy it in the short term, in the long run, overfeeding causes medical issues that can bring great suffering or shorten the life to your pet.

The slavery to the perceptions and projections of emotions fades as the heart is cleansed. When Love is conditional, the tendency is to use Love as a punishment or a weapon. When we have not realized the grandness of creation, we think that Love is a commodity that has a limited supply. We will negotiate, manipulate, and terrorize others into providing us with the Love we think we need or deserve. Once we realize that other people are not responsible for our emotions, then a relative calm comes over the outer portions of our lives. We realize all the Love we could ever need comes from the source of creation. This Love is literally all around us. Like a fish that swims in water, we live, move, and breathe in a world where everything vibrates with Love. When we develop the ability to consciously open the heart, we have the capacity to receive all the Love we need to heal wounds, to love ourselves, and to be compassionate with others.

With the top three chakras open and functioning, the student of The Grail Path understands the consequences of their actions. They know that to spread negativity will only bring negativity back to them. They know that any negativity shared by others is a reflection of an inner being that is governed by issues and negative perceptions. They also know that to participate in negativity or immoral behavior burdens the soul. We have come to realize that there are many things that happened before our awakening that now must be cleaned up. It is not smart to add to the mess by being negative or acting in immoral or mean ways. For this reason, practitioners of The Grail path strive to share only happiness and good vibes. By remaining affirmative and using the skills learned from the previous chakras, they can find positive solutions to situations and create a pleasant environment to surround themselves.

As leaders, the practitioners of The Grail Path strive to make difficult situations seem easy or fun. They use strategies to keep the mind away from negative emotions and focused on the job at hand. As a camp director, this skill was key for me. When a child got a tick, they were required to see the camp nurse to have it removed. On the trek to the nurse's office, which could take up to 15 minutes, the child was asked to name the tick and start a story about its family and how it ended up riding on its current human. Over the years, I had several adult leaders and teen councilors ask why we did this. It seemed pointless, as well as, just plain weird. I told the leaders and councilors that they were keeping the child occupied with a positive activity while walking to the nurse's office. Instead of imagining a horrible medical extraction scenario and becoming panicked that they were going to die, they were laughing and creating the whole way. Not only did the nurse have an easier time of removing the tick, but the card that the tick was placed on, complete with the tick's name, location, date, and place of origin, would get home to parents as a prized specimen. That way, if further medical intervention was needed, the parent had the tick, complete with all the pertinent information so the family doctor could test it. If the child had had a sufficiently fearful experience, the possibilities were high that the tick, with its valuable medical information, would have been ditched before getting home and the child would not come back to camp again. Scrubbing latrines, trekking to outposts in the heat, and riding out thunderstorms were accompanied with singing and silliness. We incorporated these practices into the camp day to make the best out of the situations that could create a negative emotional imprint.

The heart needs a balanced life in order for it to operate at optimum capacity. Too much noise, hard work, and stress can cause imbalances that reduce the heart's transmutation abilities. Emotional turmoil dissipates the Grace that has accrued in the spiritual system, which makes the heart weak. It is then vulnerable to every misperception and is unable to forgive or be compassionate. When practitioners of The Grail Path do not have control of their inner life or when they know that they are in one of life's negative events, they have a tendency to seclude themselves. This allows them to use all their energies to get their heart's system back on track. Another reason they seclude themselves, is to not expose others to their unbalanced or negative vibrations. They know that negativity and confusion can have the same characteristics as a virus and spread dis*ease* through a community.

Supplemental Heart Chakra Practices

1. You can supplement the basic lightwork meditation of this chakra by imagining the color green, chanting the mantra "Yam," or spinning the energy within the heart chakra to the left.

2. A spiritual practice that I used during this part of my spiritual journey was what I called, "What is Good about THIS!" practice. Every time an event, circumstance or person presented me with something that brought up negative emotions or a negative mentality, I asked myself, "What is Good about THIS!" Everything from being late to work to a child bad mouthing me became a writing prompt for my journal. It made me look deeply into the events of the day and clear the negativity that popped up. It could be that I missed being in a car accident because I was late for work. A bad day at school might be the reason for my child's hateful outburst. It was time to be grateful for the first and be compassionate with my child's distress for the second.

3. Compassion is a skill that can be learned. In the beginning, your inner temple was established in the third eye or upper tan t'ien. As you continue to work with this visualization, your inner temple will grow and eventually fill the heart. The heart has the ability to transmute not just your inner emotions, but also the emotions of others. When someone is pouring out

their sufferings on you, do not intensify the situation by piling on more emotion and drama. Actively open your heart and shine the light of your inner temple. The positive light and Grace that you pour out will neutralize and balance the negative energy that this person is spewing into the atmosphere. This will also provide you with a type of shield that will protect you from the acid of the negativity. This is how John, Mary the Mother, and Mary the Magdalene helped Jesus through his sufferings on the cross. Periodically, practice opening your inner temple and shining the Light of Grace into your environment. It will cleanse away the negativity that is in your space.

4. One way to practice opening the heart is to bless the emergency vehicles when you see or hear one. Do not worry about the what's or why's of the emergency. Open you heart and say something, either out loud or in your head, like, "May the best possible outcome come of your run today." Then, close your heart and move on with your own business.

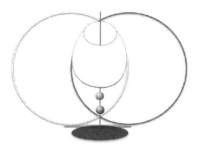

FIFTH ATTAINMENT – THE SOLAR PLEXUS

As the lightwork meditation continues, the cup grows and the light flows into the solar plexus. The solar plexus is the seat of our personal power. Personal empowerment is not about controlling others or imposing your will on every situation. Expanding the love for yourself happens when you take control of your situation. Taking control of your life through discipline and organization will go a long way toward building self-respect, self-worth, and confidence. We now add the layer of including "*Me*," my needs, and my desires into the matrix of life. The caring nature of the emotional personality, for the most part, wants what is best for others, but we cannot forget ourselves in the process. Otherwise, our lives become filled with drudgery that can lead to hopelessness.

There is a big difference between being a servant and being a slave. The servant chooses the situations and circumstances that they wish to participate in and which they do not. A slave feels as if they have no choice in the matter and is haphazardly blown around by the demands of others. The difference between these two can be as simple as a shift in attitude. When we consciously choose to give, then thoughts of being taken advantage of either fade away or cannot emerge.

Jesus tells us that if someone takes your shirt, then also give them your cloak. Or if you are required to walk a mile, then choose to walk another mile. How can choosing to give make such a big difference? This seems counterintuitive. However, I have used this mind shifting formula with great success. One day when I was eating in a local fast-food restaurant, someone stole my purse. It contained all my credit cards and ID, which I knew through much legwork, could be recovered. What I just could not shake was the issue of being violated. Someone had taken what was mine from me. It was then that I remembered what Jesus said. So, I imagined willingly giving my purse to the person. In order to accomplish even the imaginary act of giving my purse, I had to see the full circumstances of my life. The loss of this one thing, a purse, would not devastate my life. The cash in my purse was not all I had. No one in my family would go hungry due to this loss. The ID and other cards in my purse could be replaced with a few phone calls and a couple of errands. The purse itself was also replaceable. So instead of a sense of loss, this incident brought a sense of gratitude for the current circumstances in my life. The only thing that changed was the way I looked at the event. Within minutes of mentally giving my purse away, the post office called. It seems that the thief dumped my wallet with all my ID, credit cards, and checkbook in a mailbox. So, I did not have to struggle to get back all my important documents. All I actually lost was the cash and the purse itself.

Choosing what, when, and where to give requires the discipline to say, "NO." It is time to realize that we are human and have physical limitations of time and resources. In the previous chakra, we learned to love ourselves just as we are. Now, we must accept the reality that we can't be everything to everyone. Personal power comes from choice and prioritization. Empowerment is not about exerting control over others, but is about controlling the demands of others on you. When you are in charge of organizing your son's karate demonstration, do not let the book fair chairman talk you into helping her the night before. You can offer to do pre-fair organization or reminding the volunteers the week before, but you must leave the night of the fair open for your prior commitment. Be creative in negotiating ways to help. Evaluate every request for help with a view to give something of value without killing yourself in the process. I have always said that you have the right to ask me for anything as long as you give me the right to say, "No." If I am not given the right to say, "No," then the relationship is not balanced. This is the first warning sign of an unhealthy relationship, if allowed to continue, will destroy your sense self-esteem and self-worth.

The next thing we must learn is when "No" is appropriate and when it is not. There is a hierarchy of commitment that must be understood. Each level of commitment needs to have its own level of priority. Of course, immediate family will have the highest priority. Parenting a young child from the age of newborn to the age of 5 is very demanding and needs to have the highest priority of your attention and energy. Young children truly need constant attention and supervision. Meeting their needs to be loved, fed, bathed, talked to, read to, cuddled, and redirected guarantee that they will grow up to be healthy people both physically and psychologically. Children are not magically delivered by a stork or just pop up out of a cabbage patch. There were actions that brought about the birth of this new being. By participating in those actions you unconsciously chose to create a new life. When you accept the responsibility of parenthood, it makes it easier to unconditionally give. Balancing the needs of a spouse, multiple children, a home, and a job can be both challenging and rewarding.

Accepting the consequences that represent your current life and taking responsibility for the things that will make it better is the first step to empowering yourself. It's time to stop wishing and start doing. The laundry does not fold itself and the dishes do not magically jump into the dishwasher. Set a schedule of when things will be done and do your best to stick to the plan. Start small. Whites are washed on Monday and Thursday. You can incorporate spiritual benefits for yourself by listening to vibrational music that soothes the spirit or doing a ½ Minute Meditation during or between chores. Once you master the laundry, then add to the plan the cleaning of one additional room. Bathroom #1 is scrubbed on Tuesday or the guest bathroom is scrubbed on Friday. You do not have to do it all yourself either! Rounding up the troops and negotiating chores benefits everyone.

There is nothing more frustrating than having to chase down the tools of life. Brooms, scissors, and toilet paper need to have designated locations. When you see the scissors lying around in some random location, take 30 seconds and put them back in the drawer where they belong. Locate things close to where they are commonly used. If the stockpile of toilet paper is located in a hall closet, buy a toilet paper container that holds 3 rolls and stand it right next to the toilet. Then you don't have to yell for someone to bring you a roll when you are half naked and left staring at an empty tube. Not to mention that a three-year-old will have great fun filling this container while you are scrubbing the tub. Make sure each member of your household has their own things like scissors, tape and staplers. There is nothing more frustrating than to spend 30 minutes hunting through the house for something that would have taken only 3 seconds to use if it had been in its rightful place. These things seem so simple, but when the plan is set up and followed consistently, life is less stressful and can even be enjoyable.

Once you get the basics of life under control, then it is time to be brave and clean out the garage or paint the living room. With the advent of Google and YouTube, you can create or fix anything! There are thousands of articles, blogs, and how-to videos that will show you step by step how to fix, design, or organize anything. Just put in a few keywords and follow along with the pros. This will save you loads of money and is a sure fire confidence builder! Once you have mastered getting out of your comfort zone and attacking those things that you wished would magically happen, nothing can stop you. Each new challenge that enters your life becomes a puzzle to solve instead of a stressful situation that causes confusion and despair.

This chakra is also an exchange valve. The difference between the solar plexus and the throat chakra is that the energy that is exchanged through the solar plexus is the Divine Power of Kundalini. Have you ever left a conversation with someone and felt like you have been punched in the gut? That is a sure sign that someone is trying to overpower you. It is disrespect in the highest degree. Since the energy of Kundalini can cause damage to your spiritual system, those who attack your solar plexus must be confronted, avoided, or simply cut out of your life. Exchanging spiritual energy is as intimate as sex. This is why official ceremonies accompany the bonding of spiritual teacher and student. Never imagine that anyone is your teacher or your student until there is a physical conversation where both parties consent to such bonding. Energy healers also have codes of conduct regarding energy exchange. Before submitting to an energy healing, find out which energy the practitioner is using. If they don't understand that there are TWO Spiritual energies and cannot tell you which they are using, DO NOT allow them to proceed. Grace or Light that falls from the crown chakra to the base chakra is what powers the energy system of those who follow The Grail Path. Stay away from energy practitioners that use Kundalini or Fire energies. They are not bad for everyone, but they are bad for you. Do not allow anyone to force his or her energy on you without your knowledge or consent. By the same token, do not force your energy upon anyone without his or her knowledge or consent.

There will be many times when a person or group will make a request but not have the resources to give back to you. It is important that you fully think through the pros and cons before committing to this person or group. Volunteering your time, skills, and money requires that you get nothing in return. For this experience to be valuable for your inner growth you must come from a place of excess resources and have a deep desire to help or give. I spent many hours volunteering my time directing day camp, organizing the science fair, and hawking turkey legs at the local Renaissance fair. What did I get out of it besides a whole lot of hard work and headaches? I got to provide a venue for girls to create their own camp and enjoy a week in the great outdoors. I got to see elementary school children explore the world of science and inventing. I got to experience living theater complete with costuming and funny accents while providing funds for the high school band to attend parades, contests, and special events. My heart was deeply involved in all those activities and the return I received was heartfelt. During the times I was volunteering, I knew I would not be able to do much of anything else. I limited the demands of others so that I would not overextend myself. That way I could enjoy the rewards of my heart and still fulfill the needs of my home and family.

I have also volunteered in places that I would never do so again. The behavior of the group was so rude and offensive that it took months to recover enough energy to keep the house clean. They were constantly requesting, but never giving anything but drama and anxiety. I got to a point where I not only refused to help anymore, but eventually I completely walked away from that group all together. It all came down to priorities. Allowing a low priority relationship to suck the life out of you to the point where you cannot provide for the needs of your inner circle and heart-felt priorities is a sign that they have to go. You love them, but they are not good for you. It's hard to wrench yourself away because they need you so much. The best service you can provide is to make them take care of themselves. Not everyone is as kind or generous as you are. "There be sharks in the water mi' lady!" They will try to take advantage of you at every turn. The best way to preserve your dignity and self-respect is to prioritize who and what gets your time, attention, and money. When the ability to take care of your inner circle diminishes, start cutting or limiting the people and activities that are on the outermost edge or lowest rung of your priority list. Then, ruthlessly stick to that plan.

Supplemental Solar Plexus Practices

1. You can supplement the basic lightwork meditation for this chakra by imagining the color yellow, chanting the mantra "Ram," or spinning the energy within the solar plexus chakra to the left.

2. The practices that accompany this chakra include affirmations that rewrite the mental program of self-worth. Self-esteem is an inside job. Modifying your inner self-talk is an important step in empowering yourself. Create empowering phrases and say them to yourself throughout the day. Here are a few examples.

   a. I am worthy of love and abundance

   b. I am valuable and needed just the way I am

   c. I am loved by the universe and all things

   d. I am free to choose what is best for me

3. Is there a chore or activity that you despise? Make a list of reasons why you would _choose_ to do this activity. Are you scrubbing the toilet because you want it to be sanitary for yourself and others? Are you being loving to the toilet itself by keeping it clean? Did you add fun like play music or listening to a pod-cast while you scrubbed? All of these things will take the negativity out of any activity you just hate to do.

4. Setting a framework, like cleaning schedules, financial budgets, and timelines, can break the overwhelming business of life into actionable pieces. Cleaning the whole house in one go can be overwhelming and the build up of undone chores can be depressing. Choosing different chores on different days can insure that your home is never a complete pigsty.

5. Another practice is to set the priorities in your life.

   a. Who is in your inner circle?

   b. Did you include yourself and your needs in the activities of your day?

   c. Work becomes fun when you sing and dance through your chores.

6. You do not have to spend extended hours doing meditation or spiritual practices when you consciously stop every few minutes to breathe or stretch.

7. Where are the interests of your heart?

   a. Helping the homeless will not bring you any heartfelt benefit if your love is for animals or trees.

8. The workplace can be the most disrespectful place of all.

a. Do your best to choose work environments that are as beneficial to your emotional wellbeing as to your wallet.

Sixth Attainment – Sacral Chakra

As we pour more light into the spiritual system, the cup deepens and opens the sacral chakra. We enter the world of pleasure. Human nature is known to seek pleasure in order to avoid pain. As our mind becomes increasingly clear, we can hear what our body really needs. The Solar Plexus chakra taught us how to take charge of our lives. Now, we use those skills to fulfill our deepest needs. When this happens, then the minor addictions and compulsions of life cease to become substitutes for love or joy. We become aware of life's imbalances. We learn when *enough* is *enough* and that the greatest pleasure in life is balance.

Stress and fighting our compulsions increases their hold on us. The reason is that both stress and fighting is the method of increasing the Divine Power of Kundalini. Kundalini can negatively activate this chakra by increasing the fire of desires. So, noticing and accepting that you need your morning coffee or that you can't go by a donut shop without stopping is the first step in clearing these addictions. As the Divine Power of Grace increases within this chakra and cleanses it, those irritating compulsions start to fade and will eventually whither over time. Keep up your meditations, affirmations, and filling with the Light of Grace! The deeper you go within, the more power is needed to create and maintain the attainments. If we let the light fade, then those pesky addictions will come back and haunt us.

The sacral chakra is also the place of the Taoist lower tan t'ien. It is the lowest energy center and is explained as being, "like the root of the tree of life." The Japanese use the term "hara" to describe this energy center, which is considered to be the seat of one's internal energy. In the Hindu Yogic tradition, this chakra is considered to be the seat of power that nourishes the entire body.

When the Divine Power of Grace is stabilized at maximum frequency, even the need for food and sex ceases. The essence of the divine is now fulfilling all bodily needs. Saints and sages that understand the magic of spiritual energy can go days and sometimes years without food or human company. The appetites of the body are nourished by the energy of life itself.

As we continue to enhance the depths of our being, we now notice that we have different facets to our personalities. There is no one role or skill that defines us. We have the ability to adapt to different roles and situations as the moment allows. Our self-esteem is not wrapped up in a job title or the material objects we own. Our identity slowly and gently becomes detached from what we have or what we do.

Once we understand the mechanism of balance, we can slowly reinstate the small things that used to be upsetting in our lives. We can face demanding situations and know that we will not be permanently damaged. We have the skills and power to refill the coffers with Grace and return to a state of balance through conscious practice.

Supplemental Sacral Chakra Practices

1. You can supplement the basic lightwork meditation by imagining the color orange, chanting the mantra "Vam," or spinning the energy within the sacral chakra to the left.

2. The work with the inner temple helps it to expand. Continue your daily visualizations of your happy place. Imagine that it has expanded to include the Sacral Chakra with in its confines.

3. Define yourself practice.

    a. List the different facets of your life.

    b. What are the different skills you possess?

    c. Notice that no one thing can define you.

4. Make a list of things that you used to do, but no longer enjoy.

    a. What things seem to be balancing themselves.

    b. What seems to be released?

    c. Take a personal inventory of what is flowing smoothly in your life.

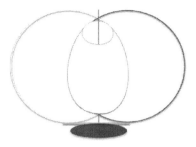

SEVENTH ATTAINMENT – BASE CHAKRA

As the Divine Power of Grace flows into the Base Chakra, the mind's eye can see the cauldron or horn of plenty. Grace has filled the entire inner being with light. It has expanded from a flat platter above the head, to a chalice, and has now become a deep bowl or cauldron. In this chakra, the base needs of security, money, and home are addressed. It is hard to feel secure and at peace when every change and moment of chaos overwhelms us with an upsurge of emotion. Before now, the addition of Grace balanced the spiritual energies and transmuted the negative emotions into positive energy. The base chakra allows us to create a solid connection to the earth via the Divine Power of Grace. The natural downward flow of Grace releases the accumulated emotional energy surrounding money and security issues into the earth. This is called "grounding." All electrical circuits, both physical and spiritual, need to be grounded so that they do not overload and explode.

Once the Divine Power of Grace is connected to the ground, struggle ends and we experience the Peace that passes all understanding. The circuit is connected and the flow of energy circulates freely. We know that the universe operates in mysterious ways that are always giving us what we need in the moment. There is always enough and we will always be provided for. It allows us to enjoy a peaceful spirit or a creative moment no matter where we are or what circumstance we find ourselves.

Supplemental Base Chakra Practices

1. You can supplement the basic lightwork meditation of this chakra by imagining the color red, chanting the crown chakra mantra "Lam," or spinning the energy within the root chakra to the left.

2. Visualize the light flowing through your body and extending from your base chakra into the ground. Imagine this light drilling deeper and deeper into the earth with each meditation. As it goes deeper into the ground, notice how the energy fans out through the earth like the roots of a tree. It is creating a sturdy foundation for your life.

3. Back-Bend Breathing Practice – Stand with feet shoulder-width apart. Place your palms on your lower back. Bend backwards slightly. Now do deep conscious breaths – in through the nose and exhale out through the mouth. As you inhale, visualize the energy above your head spinning to the left. Feel the energy flowing down the back, through the pelvis, and down the legs as you exhale.

EIGHTH ATTAINMENT – TRANSFIGURATION, COSMIC EGG, OR WHITE ROBE

When the Divine Power of Grace has completely cleansed the Base Chakra, the masculine and feminine spheres merge. We now have the ability to surround ourselves with a field of white light. The Grace now flows into the aura and turns it a soft glowing white. It is only visible to those who have the ability to see auras. The ancient Egyptians referred to this attainment as the White Robe. Egyptian Priests and Priestesses were ceremoniously enrobed in white to symbolize this high spiritual achievement. Jesus of Nazareth not only attained this status but also was able to increase the energy of his transfiguration to the point where three of his disciples could physically see it. The Buddhist tradition displays the Buddha sitting on a lotus. The white lotus symbolizes the encircling energy that defines this attainment. The Cosmic Egg is the gnostic terminology for this same achievement. Notice the chair backs and the backdrops that frame the Pope, the Dalai Lama, and the enlightened sages of India. It will most probably physically mark out the white aura that is too subtle for most people to see.

With practice, this light can be modulated to either filter or block the vibrations that emanate from the outer environment. Environments that cause great disturbances have little or no effect anymore. We now have the confidence to move into challenging situations because we are protected. There is no such thing as an invincible shield. Continued practice is required to keep this light-shield strong. However, a light-shield can be damaged or broken by extreme life events or master Kundalini practitioners. As we learned in the sacral chakra, healing can be achieved by increasing your intake of Grace. This restores the balance of spiritual energies and reconnects the flow of Grace to the ground. Once the reconnection occurs, and then the Cosmic Egg can be rebuilt.

The White Robe is a double-edged sword because it magnifies the inner disturbances. While the outer vibrations bounce off the shield, the inner vibrations reverberate within an empty room. It will be impossible for you to ignore anything that bubbles up from your subconscious. Since you now have the complete set of tools and practice regularly to keep your energies at peak levels, it is easy to deal with these moments as they arise quickly and easily.

Once you have stabilized the energy into a complete bubble that surrounds yourself, it is possible to expand this bubble to fill a room, a city, a country, the whole planet and even the cosmos. Development of this attainment can take many forms. It is from this bubble that you are able to send healings, blessings, and good vibes through the ethers to others. There are endless possibilities of benefitting the wider world with your meditations and inner energy manipulations without ever leaving your meditation mat. While there are few who reach this level of mastery, even fewer take the next step.

Supplemental Cosmic Egg Practices

1. Continue envisioning your inner temple daily. Work to expand it to the point where it completely fills the aura and encompasses your entire physical self. Instead of moving inward to find your happy place, it should now be so large that it continually surrounds you everywhere you go. The inner temple is equivalent to the light that filters or blocks the outer vibrations. We feel at peace anywhere because, like a turtle, we take our home with us wherever we go.

NINTH ATTAINMENT — IMMACULATE CONCEPTION

It would seem that our meditation has come to an end. You are now so solid in your foundations that nothing can take away the Peace that has been cultivated. The inner being has been completely cleansed by the Grace that flows through the entire being. Issues and ego can no longer gain a footing in this soul and the inner temple has grown to encompass our physical body. However, this is really just the beginning.

We learned that the spirituality of the ancients symbolized Grace as the "Semen of God." The ancient logic was that the rain from Father Sky was inseminating Mother Earth who then produced the foodstuffs from deep within her womb. It is the imagery of the divine insemination from above that leads to the mythos of a God impregnating mortal women. Since these women experience a full penetration of the Divine Masculine from above, the subsequent conception is considered divine, immaculate, or clean. Only those whose Kundalini has not arisen through the base chakra, metaphorically known as "Virgins," can experience the immaculate conception.

The divine calls the divinely inspired, *sometimes repeatedly*. They are personally recruited. They hear voices or have visions of angels that specifically solicit them to do something. A cattle call from the pulpit will not work with these people because they do not have enough ego to assume that the announcement to the group is calling them. When these people look into their past they see that every lesson, every twist of fate, has led them to this mission. In most cases, this mission is something that they would never have dreamed of doing.

This attainment is as much a choice as it is a realization. It is a complete changing of gears. We move from accepting the world as it is to actively choosing some aspect of human reality to champion or change. In many cases, these missions arise out of heart wrenching or desperate situations. The virgin now chooses to insure that no one will ever have to suffer in this way again. The "conception" does not take place until Mary the Virgin accepts her mission in life. Once The Immaculate Conception takes place, the Divine Power of Kundalini rises as the passion to complete the mission given escalates.

Instead of buckling under a burden of anguish, she moves into a phase metaphorically called "Motherhood." For a time, the mission must incubate within the soul. Knowledge is collected. Networks are created. Every facet of the personality that was previously developed is now used to further the mission. There are many prophets in the Bible, like Jonah, who were told to give a message but instead they got on a boat going the opposite direction. If you are called and do not answer, life will throw you back on your path until you accept.

Where as before we were not defined by any job or any relationship, now we narrow our focus for the rest of our lives to one purpose. Mary was well aware of the dangers she faced, not just from the physical complications of birth but also from the Jewish law. She had a surety of faith that demonstrated the strength of Grace that circulated through her spiritual system. She spent the rest of her life in the service of this divine mission, which continued after the crucifixion when Jesus designated John to now be her son.

The Buddha and Mohammed were both commanded by the divine to take this next step. Jesus' last words to his disciples were to go out and preach the word. Even today, the current Dali Lama has issued orders to many Rinpoches to exit their mediation caves or to actively prolong their lives in order to come out into the world to teach the next generation all they know. It is not enough to cleanse the soul and be a beneficial presence in the world. It is important that once your reach a high level of mastery that you help others to achieve this same level of attainment. What good is a lifetime of knowledge that removes human suffering if you do not pass it on?

The cosmos is made up of many facets. The spiritual realm is just one facet of the cosmos. The environment, science, healing arts, political and race relations are just a few of the facets that need visionaries, masters, and ambassadors. These areas of our world need people to step out into the fray of life and pass down their knowledge to make the world a better place. The ancients considered anything that was active and operated in the physical world as male. Any divinely inspired mission that actively and positively changes the world can be considered a first born son. Every cause like breast cancer's pink ribbon campaign, MADD, the non-violent demonstrations for equality, and environmental issues like saving the rain forest is a male child that was conceived out of despair.

Supplemental Immaculate Conception Practices

1. There is no practice for this attainment. The Immaculate Conception is something that just happens. It cannot be forced in any way. Anything that you consciously work to create is pure ego. The Immaculate Conception can only take place within a soul that has been completely cleansed of ego. Just continue with your practices that fill the inner being with Grace.

Tenth Attainment - Birth of the Divine Child, Mustard Seed, Pearl of Great Price, Stone from Heaven

As Grace continues to flow into a fully enlightened spiritual system, the excess divine energy settles into the bottom of the cup and creates a physical form that can only be seen in the mind's eye. In the book of Matthew, Jesus tells of a mustard seed that is very small but when it is full grown, it becomes a tree. It can also look like a white pearl or a white stone. There are many fables concerning the pearl of great price and the white stone that falls from heaven.

Another interpretation of the coalescing of the Divine Power of grace is the birth of the Divine Child. This child will be born and inhabit your inner temple. He will grow as your mission gains power and momentum. Set backs will cause the divine child to reverse in age, but balance can be restored by ramping up the practices that bring more Grace into the spiritual system. As the Divine Power of Grace is the essence of God the Father, this baby is always male. As this boy grows, your masculine qualities of logic, order, and discipline grow too. In this way, you saturate your inner being with masculine qualities from within. Discipline is slowly and naturally incorporated into life, one step at a time. It is not inflicted upon yourself with shame and force. We now see why Jesus' statement that he will make her, Mary the Magdalene, male has meaning.

The Taoist tradition states that the birth of the divine child takes place in the lower tan t'ien. Christian tradition concurs with its story of Jesus being born in the "stable," or lowest level of the typical Middle Eastern home.

Supplemental Divine Child Practices

1. Your divine child will need all the same care that is given to a physical child. When you perform your happy place meditations include feeding, cuddling, playing and educating your divine child. How will you know if this child is really more than a figment of your imagination? There is one test that confirms a true divine birth. Every time you kiss this child, it is your cheek that feels like it has been kissed. When you feed this child, it is your belly that feels full. When you play games with this child, it is your spirit that feels uplifted.

2. The other practice that grows your divine child is to work on your divinely inspired mission. Everyday, do something that moves that mission forward.

MEN OF THE GRAIL

The symbols of the star, water, and a silvery essence are properties that bring balance and wholeness to the female nature. Yet, literature sings the praises and archeology has unearthed men who boast the qualities of Grace. Kings and warriors that are said to be filled with the Divine Power of Grace, or to metaphorically possess the Holy Grail, have come full circle in their spiritual journey. The Grail Path is the secondary path for those who must first kill the ego. These are extraordinary men who have achieved the understanding of both spiritual paths.

The most notable archeological find was the Egyptian pharaoh Psusennes I. Professor Pierre Montet found Psusennes I's intact tomb in 1940. Psusennes, which means "The Star Appearing in the City," ruled from Tanis under the throne name that meant, "Great are the Manifestations of Ra. Chosen of Amun." Psusennes' outer and middle sarcophagi were gold because they were recycled from previous burials through the state sanctioned activity of tomb robbing. However, the innermost or personal casket was made of silver. The archeologists have dubbed Psusennes I the 'Silver Pharaoh.' The cartouche of Psusennes features a star, loaf of bread, water, and a kite (an Egyptian white bird that can be equated with a Christian dove) hovering over or to the side of the hieroglyph for city. I'd say they covered all the bases to describe that this man was filled with Grace.

Ancient Persia's Cyrus the Great is another man who touted his connection to the Divine Power of Grace. The subjects of both his native and conquered peoples referred to Cyrus as "The Father" during his lifetime. When he liberated the Jews from Babylon, his just and benevolent rule gained Cyrus the title of Messiah or Anointed One. Cyrus is the only Gentile to be given this title in the Hebrew Bible. To further cement the claim of divinely appointed leader, Cyrus constructed the earliest *Paradisia* or garden confirmed by archeological evidence. Cyrus' garden is believed to be patterned after the celestial garden of four rivers, which is also the model used in the Bible for the Garden of Eden. The ancient Persian Kings considered the title "Gardener" to be the highest honor. The ancients believed that only God the Father had control of the water that could magically make the desert bloom.

Joseph of Arimathea is featured in the New Testament as the man who recovered Jesus' dead body from the Cross. In the few lines that are dedicated to Joseph, we are told that he was a prominent member of the High Council, he had hollowed out his own rock tomb, and he graciously placed Jesus' dead body into this newly finished tomb. How did the legend that Joseph was the keeper of the Grail develop? The Bible does not say that Joseph used a cup to catch the blood of the dying Jesus. Joseph is not mentioned at the Last Supper. How could he have obtained the cup that Jesus used to perform the first Eucharist?

In order to unravel this mystical puzzle, we must know some basic facts about The Hero's Journey. The Hero's Journey uses Kundalini to cut away the encrusted ego. The Holy Spear is the object that is created in the mind's eye as the Kundalini rises through the chakras. The transformation process creates a dark emptiness that allows the consciousness to expand. The ancients nicknamed this process of spiritual transformation, *"hollowing out the tomb."* So, this little bit of information tells us a lot about Joseph. He was an advanced practitioner of The Hero's Journey. He had completed his tomb, which meant that he metaphorically possessed the Holy Spear. His ego was officially dead and he was waiting for The Divine Power of Grace to fill his inner being. We have to remember that, at birth, Jesus was proclaimed as the Prince of Peace. The metaphorical connotation of this title is that Jesus was considered to be Grace incarnate. So, when Joseph puts Jesus' body in his freshly hollowed out tomb, what his is doing is filling his inner being with Grace. Today we would say, "put Jesus in your heart." Another euphemism is to say that this is the Second Coming of Christ. The first coming was the arising of the

Divine Power of Kundalini, which creates the tomb, and the second coming is the filling of the empty tomb with the Divine Power of Grace. As we have seen, the filling of the inner being with Grace creates a chalice in the mind's eye. Once you can see the cup in your imagination, then you metaphorically possess The Holy Grail. This is how Joseph of Arimathea came to possess both the Holy Spear and the Holy Grail. Neither is a physical object. They are both spiritual attainments. From here, the legends get very creative with far off locations while mixing in a bit of metaphorical layering to enhance the spiritual understanding of the story.

The Epic of Gilgamesh is the oldest piece of literature that uses the literary format of The Hero's Journey. The first few words of the text read, *Sha naqba īmuru,* which means "He who Saw the Deep." This alone tells the reader that they are to look deeper. That this is a metaphorical tale. The first half of Gilgamesh's journey deals with subduing, befriending, and killing of the ego. The common metaphor for initiating this process is Hieros Gamos. After the Ego dies, Gilgamesh partakes in a second quest, the search for immortality. He eventually finds the Old Man Utnapishtim who tells him the story of the great flood. So again, the ego dies and the inner being is filled with water, which is a prominent symbol of Grace. While Gilgamesh does not escape death, he does achieve an inner happiness and joy that lasts for the rest of his days.

King Arthur and Knights of the Round Table was a tale created by a monk in the middle ages. Here again, we have a tale that is built upon the scaffolding of mystical transformation. Only a knight can go on a Grail Quest. We have learned the dangers of mixing and matching the Divine Energies. Requiring full knighthood corroborates that completion of the primary path must take place before attempting the secondary spiritual path. This guarantees that that you will not mix the Divine Energies and cause great harm to your inner being. Knights that have dis-*Graced* themselves can never attain the grail because the Divine Power of Grace creates the grail. No Grace means there can be no Grail.

One of the jobs of the chivalrous knight is to rescue damsels in distress. What is it that seems to always be distressing the damsels? A dragon is the usual culprit. One of the common symbols for the Divine

Power of Kundalini is the snake or dragon. By slaying the dragon, the knight brings Peace to the maiden, who is then awakened to her spiritual gifts with a kiss. So maybe, the princess fairy tales like *Sleeping Beauty* have a little more substance than we previously thought.

FINAL WARNING

We have seen that The Grail Path is designed to bring enlightenment to the creative-emotional person. What happens when an intellectual person follows The Grail Path without killing the ego first? The consequences are as dire as a creative-emotional person who follows The Hero's Journey before they are able to control the emotions.

The intellectual person begins the spiritual journey with an excess of Grace. When more Grace is poured into the spiritual system, the overload of Grace blends with the negative side effects of an encrusted ego. This leads to a narrowing of thought patterns into judgment and condemnation. The goal of The Hero's Journey is to increase the Kundalini in the spiritual system in order to expand the consciousness or open the mind. Opening the mind along with the warming of the heart brings caring and compassion to the intellect.

When Grace is poured into an encrusted ego, the judgments and condemnations contract and become hardened even further. Negative thoughts are engrained even deeper. The arrogance of knowing what is good and bad, as evidenced by the actions of Hitler, can become so heinous that killing those who do not fit a specific profile invokes no emotional regret. Today, we call these people psychopaths. They have no emotions. They seek only for their own benefit. They use and abuse things, people, and the environment without remorse. The ancients assigned these qualities to the archetype of Lucifer. Lucifer is the morning star, but his light is cold, arrogant, selfish, and ultimately destructive.

ABOUT THE AUTHOR

Mischa V Alyea has done everything from developing an inventing workshop as the elementary science fair coordinator to directing Day Camp for 300 girls to refinishing the wood floors in her home. She is also an accomplished seamstress, cake decorator, and DIYer.

Mischa was introduced to meditation in 1998. With three children, multiple volunteer positions, and most recently two family weddings she does not know how she could have survived such a diverse chaotic life without meditation. She makes time every day to meditate.

Now that the children are grown and settled in their own lives, Mischa founded Aashni Spiritual Living. She writes and publishes books on meditation and mystical transformation.

Mischa lives in Kansas City with her husband, Tom, and Sushi the infamous House Monster.

Visit us at:

www.AashniSpiritualLiving.com

Other Books by:
Mischa V Alyea

Over 50 different
1/2 Minute Meditations
to keep your energy flowing
through the day.

www.AashniSpiritualLiving.com

We invite you to select your next
meditation journal from our growing line
of products for meditation enthusiasts

 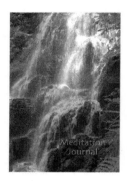

Visit our website for a complete listing
www.AashniSpiritualLiving.com/Journals

Made in the USA
San Bernardino, CA
02 November 2015